EASTERN PHILOSOPHY

THE BASICS

Eastern Philosophy: The Basics is an essential introduction to major Indian and Chinese philosophies, both past and present. Exploring familiar metaphysical and ethical questions from the perspectives of different eastern philosophies, including Confucianism, Daoism, and strands of Buddhism and Hinduism, this book covers key figures, issues, methods and concepts. Questions discussed include:

- What is the 'self'?
- Is human nature inherently good or bad?
- How is the mind related to the world?
- How can you live an authentic life?
- What is the fundamental nature of reality?

With timelines highlighting key figures and their contributions, a list of useful websites and further reading suggestions for each topic, this engaging overview of fundamental ideas in eastern philosophy is valuable reading for all students of philosophy and religion, especially those seeking to understand eastern perspectives.

Victoria S. Harrison is Reader in Philosophy at the University of Glasgow, UK. She has extensive experience of teaching Indian and Chinese philosophies at undergraduate level in both the UK and the USA.

The Basics

ACTING
BELLA MERLIN

ANTHROPOLOGY
PETER METCALF

ARCHAEOLOGY (SECOND EDITION)
CLIVE GAMBLE

ART HISTORY
GRANT POOKE AND DIANA NEWALL

ARTIFICIAL INTELLIGENCE
KEVIN WARWICK

THE BIBLE
JOHN BARTON

BUDDHISM
CATHY CANTWELL

CONTEMPORARY LITERATURE
SUMAN GUPTA

CRIMINAL LAW
JONATHAN HERRING

CRIMINOLOGY (SECOND EDITION)
SANDRA WALKLATE

DANCE STUDIES
JO BUTTERWORTH

ECONOMICS (SECOND EDITION)
TONY CLEAVER

EDUCATION
KAY WOOD

EVOLUTION
SHERRIE LYONS

EUROPEAN UNION (SECOND EDITION)
ALEX WARLEIGH-LACK

FILM STUDIES
AMY VILLAREJO

FINANCE (SECOND EDITION)
ERIK BANKS

HUMAN GENETICS
RICKI LEWIS

HUMAN GEOGRAPHY
ANDREW JONES

INTERNATIONAL RELATIONS
PETER SUTCH AND JUANITA ELIAS

ISLAM (SECOND EDITION)
COLIN TURNER

JOURNALISM STUDIES
MARTIN CONBOY

JUDAISM
JACOB NEUSNER

LANGUAGE (SECOND EDITION)
R. L. TRASK

LAW
GARY SLAPPER AND DAVID KELLY

LITERARY THEORY (SECOND EDITION)
HANS BERTENS

LOGIC
J. C. BEALL

MANAGEMENT
MORGEN WITZEL

MARKETING (SECOND EDITION)
KARL MOORE AND NIKETH PAREEK

MEDIA STUDIES
JULIAN MCDOUGALL

PHILOSOPHY (FOURTH EDITION)
NIGEL WARBURTON

PHYSICAL GEOGRAPHY
JOSEPH HOLDEN

POETRY (SECOND EDITION)
JEFFREY WAINWRIGHT

POLITICS (FOURTH EDITION)
STEPHEN TANSEY AND NIGEL JACKSON

THE OLYMPICS
ANDY MIAH & BEATRIZ GARCIA

THE QUR'AN
MASSIMO CAMPANINI

RACE AND ETHNICITY
PETER KIVISTO AND PAUL R. CROLL

RELIGION (SECOND EDITION)
MALORY NYE

RELIGION AND SCIENCE
PHILIP CLAYTON

RESEARCH METHODS
NICHOLAS WALLIMAN

ROMAN CATHOLICISM
MICHAEL WALSH

SEMIOTICS (SECOND EDITION)
DANIEL CHANDLER

SHAKESPEARE (THIRD EDITION)
SEAN MCEVOY

SOCIOLOGY
KEN PLUMMER

SOCIAL WORK
MARK DOEL

SPECIAL EDUCATIONAL NEEDS
JANICE WEARMOUTH

TELEVISION STUDIES
TOBY MILLER

TERRORISM
JAMES M. LUTZ AND BRENDA J. LUTZ

THEATRE STUDIES
ROBERT LEACH

WORLD HISTORY
PETER N. STEARNS

EASTERN PHILOSOPHY
THE BASICS

Victoria S. Harrison

Routledge
Taylor & Francis Group
LONDON AND NEW YORK

First published 2013
by Routledge
2 Park Square, Milton Park, Abingdon, Oxon OX14 4RN

Simultaneously published in the USA and Canada
by Routledge
711 Third Avenue, New York, NY 10017

Routledge is an imprint of the Taylor & Francis Group, an informa business

British Library Cataloguing in Publication Data
A catalogue record for this book is available from the British Library

Library of Congress Cataloging in Publication Data
Harrison, Victoria S.
Eastern philosophy : the basics / Victoria S. Harrison.
pages cm – (The basics)
Includes bibliographical references and index.
1. Philosophy, Asian. I. Title.
B121.H37 2012
181–dc23
2012005538

ISBN: 978-0-415-58732-7 (hbk)
ISBN: 978-0-415-58733-4 (pbk)
ISBN: 978-0-203-10337-1 (ebk)

Typeset in Bembo
by Taylor & Francis Books

MIX
Paper from responsible sources
FSC
www.fsc.org
FSC® C004839

Printed and bound in Great Britain by
TJ International Ltd, Padstow, Cornwall

For Rhett Gayle, intrepid adventurer of the mind.

CONTENTS

FIGURES AND TABLES

FIGURES

TABLES

Every effort has been made to trace the owners of the copyright to the image reproduced in Figure 5.2.

ACKNOWLEDGEMENTS

A book such as this one is built upon the accomplishments of others and it is impossible to acknowledge all of the debts incurred in the construction process. However, especial thanks are due to my colleague Richard E. King, whose work I have relied on extensively in Chapters 1–3. I also owe a special debt of gratitude to Philip J. Ivanhoe for his encouragement and his comments on Chapter 6; and to my husband, Rhett Gayle, for his ability to clarify an idea no matter what its original cultural home. I am grateful to each of these philosophers for saving me from stumblingly blindly into a number of conceptual pitfalls. That I have surely failed to avoid others is entirely my own responsibility.

INTRODUCTION

Over time and across cultures human ingenuity, combined with curiosity, has given rise to a rich array of philosophies – more or less abstract and systematic ways of understanding ourselves and the world we inhabit. Amongst this diversity a distinction is commonly made between western philosophy, which traces its pedigree to a group of ancient Greek thinkers active before the Common Era, and eastern philosophy, which does not. This book is concerned with eastern philosophy.

WHAT IS 'EASTERN PHILOSOPHY'?

Although many of the ideas discussed in this book are very old, some dating back over two thousand years, the convention of classifying them together under one heading – whether 'eastern philosophy', 'Asian philosophy' or 'oriental philosophy' – is a product of nineteenth-century western scholarship. Prior to modern times no one in India, China, Japan or Korea would have recognized any of those terms as identifying a unique object of study. Nonetheless these terms are now commonly used; although, due to increased sensitivity to the vice of 'orientalism' in the post-colonial era (Said 2003), since the late twentieth century the former two have often been preferred to 'oriental philosophy'.

Employing a term such as 'eastern philosophy' emphasizes a contrast between the philosophy of the European tradition (with its extensions into America and Australasia) and non-European philosophy. This way of framing the relationship between the world's philosophies – in terms of two categories, European (western) and non-European (eastern) – gives the misleading impression that 'eastern philosophy' is a single homogeneous tradition. This is unhelpful because, in focusing our minds on a supposed clear-cut contrast between 'eastern' and 'western' philosophies, attention is drawn away from the details of the distinct philosophical systems of Asia. If we focus instead on these details we will find ourselves confronted by philosophies that developed not only across broad sweeps of time but also across a huge environmentally diverse land mass that has been host to an array of political, religious and cultural systems colouring the intellectual life of specific regions in distinctive ways.

A further problem invited by use of the term 'eastern philosophy' is that it can suggest that the geographical and ideological boundaries between 'East' and 'West' are easily identifiable rather than largely a matter of perspective (Figure 0.1). To the Chinese, India is 'West' and, in fact, from a philosophical point of view, the philosophies of India are more akin to those that flourished in the 'West' than to those that have been prominent in China (on the shared heritage of Indian and 'western' philosophies, see McEvilley 2002).

So this book, despite its title, is really about *philosophy in Asia* rather than *eastern philosophy*. It is premised on the idea that there is no such thing as eastern philosophy, if what we mean by that is a unified philosophical tradition growing from a common root (in the way that European philosophy, despite later diversity, is rooted in the Hellenic tradition). This book will introduce you to a number of distinctive philosophical systems which evolved in different cultural and temporal contexts as people sought intellectual responses to the questions that puzzled them.

Given this understanding of the material, the selection of what to include and exclude will inevitably be contentious. It would be impossible for a short book such as this to cover all the traditions that have at one time or another been regarded as part of 'eastern philosophy'. Readers might wonder, for example, why Islamic philosophy is not included. Briefly, that choice was made because regarding Islamic philosophy as one of the philosophies unique

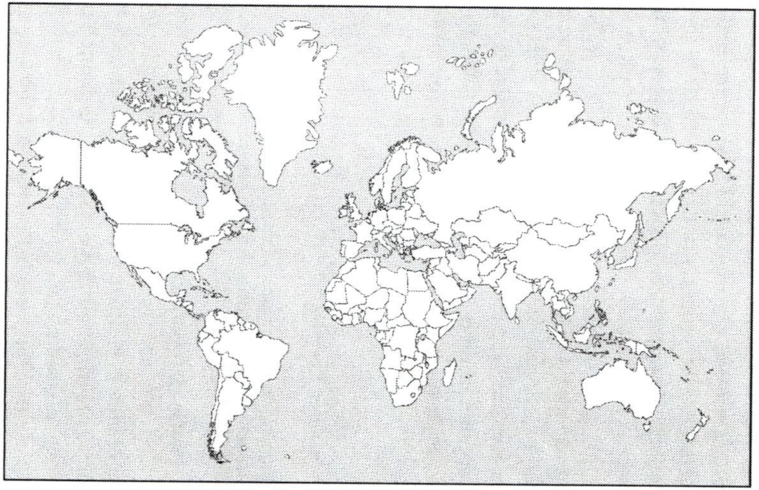

Figure 0.1 Where would you draw the boundary between 'West' and 'East'?

to Asia is especially hard to sustain given that it is rooted in the same Hellenic tradition as European philosophy (Fakhry 2004). This book focuses on certain of the philosophies that developed in India and China because, in each case, the roots of the traditions to be examined are found in non-Hellenic cultures. Moreover, the striking differences between the philosophies of India and those of China, as well as the diversity of philosophical systems found within each area, will support my claim that 'eastern philosophy' is a spurious category. Other authorial choices could have been made, but the field is such that blunt decisions cannot be avoided.

This book unapologetically concentrates on classical Indian philosophy and classical Chinese philosophy. This is because, with only a few exceptions – Islamic philosophy being one – all the major philosophies that were formative of Asian cultures developed from these two philosophical roots: the Vedic root in India and the Sinitic root in China. In explaining the 'basics' of these ancient and internally complex philosophies, this book guides the reader through a range of distinctive and insightful ways of thinking about the world and our place within it.

PHILOSOPHY AS A CROSS-CULTURAL PHENOMENON

Another principle used in selecting material for inclusion in this book is that the ideas and arguments discussed here should be recognizable as philosophy. This, of course, presupposes that there is an activity called 'philosophizing' that we can recognize across cultural and temporal distances. The reader is warned that this may turn out to be the most contentious claim made in this book, and it cannot be fully defended in the space available here.

Fortunately, the assertion that philosophy is practised by people within different cultures (and in different times) does not commit us to the further claim that exactly the same thing is being practised in these widely different contexts. So we do not need to defend the latter claim in order to hold the former. Ludwig Wittgenstein (1959) used the example of games to explain the idea that by means of 'family resemblances' we can recognize different things as belonging to the same category even in cases where there is no single feature that they all share (baseball and solitaire, for example, are both games but they lack a common feature). This idea is now routinely used to explain the relationship between religions (Harrison 2007: chapter 2). However, it can also provide us with a framework to think about the relationship between different world philosophies. If we drop the idea that 'philosophy' must have a single defining feature – a common methodology, for example – wherever it appears, we open the way for regarding philosophies as existing in different varieties that are coloured by the cultural conditions in which they developed and matured. Some philosophies have more in common than others, and some may have very little in common. But the fact that the world's philosophies lack a single common feature – if it is a fact – need not perturb us. We do not need such a feature to determine whether a specific tradition should count as 'philosophical' or not, instead we can rely on being able to spot overlapping family resemblances.

This family resemblance model opens the way for the practice of global philosophy by allowing us to recognize different traditions as *philosophical* without requiring us to give any one of them a pre-eminent position as the paradigm case against which to judge all others. It also counteracts the temptation to regard intellectual traditions as monolithic 'isms', thereby allowing us to appreciate the real transformations they undergo over time and in different cultural environments. A further virtue of the family resemblance model is that it provides us with a perspective from which to view the similarities and the differences between traditions, without pushing us to emphasize one at the expense of the other. Nonetheless, the model is not without its critics and the notion of global philosophy which it underpins remains something of a Holy Grail among current practitioners of the discipline known as **comparative philosophy** (see Appendix 2 for an explanation of the convention employed here, briefly when a word or phrase appears in bold typeface it can be looked up in the online *Stanford Encyclopedia of Philosophy*). I return to these issues in the concluding chapter.

The last thing to say here about the claim that we can recognize the practice of philosophy across different cultures and times is that the proof of the pudding will be in the eating. After considering the material presented in the chapters of this book, readers will be able to judge for themselves whether the Indian and Chinese thinkers examined here were engaging in an activity that can properly be called philosophy.

PHILOSOPHICAL QUESTIONS

Studying the forms that philosophy has taken in Asia often involves getting to grips with ideas which are unlikely to be part of your natural way of thinking. Nonetheless, the questions which typically concern philosophers are remarkably similar wherever and whenever they are found: 'What is the self?', 'What is the best way to live?', 'Where do we come from?' and 'What happens when we die?'. These questions have interested philosophers from all times and cultures; and that really shouldn't surprise us, because they are the same questions that everyone ponders in their more reflective moments. We might say that these questions arise directly from the human condition. Recognizing that the same questions are asked across cultural and temporal boundaries helps to breakdown the idea that the people in the world can be divided into 'us' and 'them', or those from the 'West' and those from the 'East'.

This book does not follow a historical pathway through the various philosophies considered; instead it is organized around certain key questions. By focusing on questions my goal is to introduce readers to the traditions considered here as *philosophies*, rather than simply as the objects of intellectual history. By providing a question-oriented guide through the philosophical engagements that took place within and across the various schools of classical Indian and Chinese thought, this book portrays them as dynamic and resourceful philosophical traditions. Many of the questions addressed will be familiar to students of western philosophy (for example, 'Should an ethical person be impartial?'). The book will show how such familiar questions are treated from unfamiliar philosophical perspectives. By creating a bridge between different perspectives, the book also draws attention to the relevance of the philosophies of Asia to contemporary global concerns.

We begin with a brief introduction to the philosophies of India; this will be followed by a similarly brief introduction to the philosophies of China.

PHILOSOPHY IN INDIA

Just as there is no such thing as eastern philosophy, there is no such thing as Indian philosophy – if we mean by that a homogeneous philosophical tradition. Instead there are a number of 'schools' of philosophy ('*darśana*' in Sanskrit, a word which is derived from the verb 'to see'), each providing a different way of looking at the nature of reality and the self. Some of them, but by no means all, are within the Hindu tradition. Despite their differing religious allegiances and varying philosophical commitments, all the schools are conventionally classified under the umbrella term 'Indian philosophy' because of their common origin in the cultural nexus of ancient India, to which we now turn.

ORIGINS AND SACRED TEXTS

Although scholars agree that there was a sophisticated urban civilization in the Indus Valley which flourished from about 2500 to 1800 BCE, the early history of India is not well understood. There are large gaps in the historical and archaeological records and hence there is little agreement about key dates. The best advice is to treat all ancient dates as speculative (this also applies to the timelines in Appendix 1).

Hinduism is often described as the world's oldest known religious tradition (Flood 1996). In fact it is a set of related traditions whose origins can be traced back to ancient times. The term 'Hinduism' is used to identify those philosophical and religious traditions that recognize the authority of certain sacred texts from what is known as the Brahmanical or Vedic Period (1500–300 BCE). All of these texts, from the *Ṛg Veda* to the *Upaniṣads*, are known as *Vedas* ('*veda*' is a Sanskrit word which means 'knowledge'). They are referred to by the term '*śruti*', which can be translated as 'what is heard'. This tells us that the origin of these texts was thought to lie in what was heard by ancient seers. Traditionally the texts themselves are thought not to have had an author, either human or divine, but to have existed eternally in a form prior to the written one in which we know them today.

The first four *Vedas* are regarded as the most sacred and these are the oldest texts of the ancient Vedic religion, a religion based on a complex sacrificial and ritual system (Zaehner 1966). Of the *Vedas*, the *Ṛg Veda* is the most ancient. It is composed of ten books, the oldest of which are thought to be books 2 and 7. These ten books inform us about Vedic culture and religious practice. While focusing on the practicalities of ritual and sacrifice, they also contain philosophical speculations on the origins of life. *Ṛg Veda* 10.129, which we consider in Chapter 2, is the most famous of these more speculative passages. It ends on a note of resigned mystery – with the admission that perhaps deep questions about cosmic origins are unanswerable. This passage is often identified as marking the beginning of the Indian sceptical tradition. Another element which became very important in the later tradition can be traced back to this section of the *Ṛg Veda*, and that is theism – the belief in the existence of a God. This belief became central to a number of philosophies which developed much later (see *Ṛg Veda* 10.82, 10.90).

At the end of the Vedic Period the *Upaniṣads* were put into written form, originally as appendages to different *Vedas*. The root meaning of the term '*Upaniṣad*' is 'to sit down near'. This refers to the ancient practice of sitting oneself down near a teacher to listen to his teachings. Nowadays, the *Upaniṣads* are probably the most well-known texts from this period. They contain more abstract philosophical reflection than the earlier texts and so reveal a transitional phase away from the concerns of the ancient Vedic religion towards an interest in the inner life (Brereton 1990). We consider the *Upaniṣads* in Chapter 2.

Those philosophical schools and religious traditions that regard the *Vedas* as authoritative are called *āstika* (affirmer), and those that do not, principally, Buddhists, Cārvākas and Jainas, are called *nāstika* (non-affirmer). The emergence of the *nāstika* traditions was roughly contemporary with the end of the Vedic Period. The distinction between affirming and non-affirming (or orthodoxy and heterodoxy) concerns a school's stance towards the *Vedas* and has nothing to do with belief in a God or gods (King 1999: chapter 3). In fact, four *darśanas* are explicitly non-theistic: Cārvāka and Buddhist, which are non-affirmers, and Mīmāṁsā and Sāṁkhya, which are affirmers (Dasti 2012).

In response to the rise of the non-Vedic systems in the fifth century BCE, the *āstika* thinkers systematized the often highly mythological, and sometimes contradictory, sayings found in the *Vedas*. In doing so they inevitably went beyond what was already given in the Vedic tradition; and this process gave rise to a number of competing *āstika darśanas*.

Śruti and *śmrti*

After the *Upaniṣads* no further writings are regarded as *śruti* (revealed truths). Later writings are classified as *śmrti*, which means 'memory'. The idea is that the later texts contain what has been remembered by the community and passed on. The well-known epic poems the *Mahābhārata* and the *Rāmāyana* are in this category. Both probably originated well before the Common Era, although they reached their final forms between 350 and 500 CE.

The *Mahābhārata* contains the *Bhagavad-gītā* (Song of the Lord, *c.*200 BCE). If you have read only one Hindu text, it is most likely to have been this one. It contains a famous dialogue between the warrior Arjuna, a nobleman and the god Krishna, who is disguised as a charioteer. Arjuna wants to withdraw from an impending battle to avoid the apparently senseless slaughter it will involve. Krishna persuades him otherwise, arguing that a man should always do his duty, and what one's duty is depends on one's class. Because Arjuna belonged to the *kṣatriya* (warrior) class, it was his duty to go into battle. The message is that one's duty should be done regardless of the consequences or of one's motivations.

The *Bhagavad-gītā* has been enormously influential on Hindu religious practice due to its emphasis on devotion to a personal god. The god in question is Krishna who is described as an avatar (incarnation) of Vishnu. The text encourages devotees to seek an intimate relationship with god. This focus on the deity gave rise to various forms of theistic monism which are linked to pivotal philosophical developments. When we consider Advaita Vedānta, in Chapter 2, you'll see that the *Bhagavad-gītā* is regarded as one of its foundational texts.

PHILOSOPHICAL DEVELOPMENTS

The Common Era saw the beginning of what is now widely regarded as the classical period of philosophy in India (*circa* the second to the twelfth century CE). During this period many philosophical perspectives, both *āstika* and *nāstika*, competed with each other. In the *āstika* camp, six distinct *darśanas* were prominent. Each was the development of a tradition stretching back into antiquity and basing itself on a particular section or theme of the *Vedas*.

The essential ideas of these *darśanas* were encapsulated in texts called *Sūtras*. '*Sūtra*' literally means 'thread' or 'strand', and refers to the thread or strand of ideas which the text endorses. The texts themselves are collections of aphorisms (a single aphorism is also known as a *sūtra*) in which the key philosophical insights of a particular school are delivered, often with breathtaking concision. *Sūtras* are multilayered texts which are the product of many generations of oral transmission from teachers to students. Most of them reached their final form in the third century BCE. Originally the aphorisms served to aid memorization of the unwritten parts of a teaching, the idea being that upon reading a particular aphorism the meaning which one had been taught will also be brought to mind. However, in time the *Sūtras* became the starting point for further philosophical reflections as different meanings were read into and out of them. This process generated a further type of literature – the commentary (*bhāṣya*). During the classical period, the *darśanas* developed as traditions of commentarial interpretation based on particular *Sūtras*. There are six *āstika darśanas* and we will meet them again in the following chapters, but it will be helpful to introduce them here. They are conventionally grouped into pairs, so that is how I will present them.

The first pair, Nyāya (the school of logic) and Vaiśeṣika (the school of atomism), represent what has been called the 'empirico-logical' strand of Hindu culture. Their foundational texts are the *Nyāya Sūtra* (third century CE) and the *Vaiśeṣika Sūtra* (third–second century BCE). These *darśanas* form a pair because their interests complement each other. They are the most analytic of the *āstika* schools and their development was interwoven to such an extent that by the eleventh century CE they seem to have merged. We return to the Nyāya in Chapter 1 and to the Vaiśeṣika in Chapter 2.

The second pair of *āstika darśanas* consists of Sāṁkhya (the school of dualistic discrimination) and Yoga (the school of classical yoga). These are the philosophical expression of the tendency within Hindu culture to seek liberation through the pursuit of pure consciousness. Their foundational texts are the *Sāṁkhya Kārikā* (fourth–fifth century CE) and the *Yoga Sūtra* (third century CE). We consider these schools in Chapter 2.

The final pair of *āstika darśanas* is formed by Mīmāṁsā (the school of Vedic exegesis) and Vedānta (the school based upon the end of the *Vedas*, i.e. the *Upaniṣads*). These schools are similar in that they are both grounded in an interpretation of the *Vedas*. Their foundational texts are the *Pūrva Mīmāṁsā Sūtra* (third century CE) and the *Vedānta* or *Brahma Sūtra* (first century CE). We will concentrate on the second of these two schools because it has been the most influential (see Chapters 2 and 3). Through the work of scholars such as Sarvepalli Radhakrishnan (1888–1975), in recent times the Vedānta *darśana* has enjoyed more global influence than any other form of Vedic philosophy.

The six *darśanas* mentioned above are, as I have explained, all within the Hindu tradition. Despite this no single one of them can be aptly described as representing the philosophy of Hinduism. Instead each provides a distinctive philosophical perspective (a *darśana*) that has arisen through systematic reflection on the *Vedas*. Although the philosophical schools that flourished in India often – although by no means always – address religious topics, they are not neatly matched to religious movements. There was no Vaiśeṣika or Nyāya form of Hinduism, for example. For this reason many of the arguments developed by philosophers in these schools are relevant to questions that go far beyond those raised by Indian religions.

Now, this introduction to the different philosophies of India would not be complete without mention of the three most influential non-Vedic, *nāstika*, traditions that developed as philosophical sparring partners to the Vedic schools.

The Cārvāka *darśana* is unusual for its materialism, hedonism and scepticism. Each of these commitments ensured that it stood out among rival perspectives in ancient and classical India. As mentioned earlier, the Cārvākas were atheists. As 'non-affirmers', they were also outspoken opponents of the Brahmanical religious authorities that defended the *Vedas*. This school is a prominent counter-example to the once common assumption that 'philosophy' in India is really just religion under another name. We examine some of their views in the following three chapters.

Jainism is perhaps the most ancient *darśana* native to the Indian subcontinent. Jaina philosophy is atheistic and, like Cārvākas, Jainas reject the *Vedas* and Brahmanical traditions. Their philosophy is characterized by a commitment to non-violence, which extends to all life-forms, including plants. As we shall see in Chapter 1, Jainas made significant contributions to the development of **logic** and the theory of knowledge.

Buddhism is a complex religious tradition that developed alongside and in conversation with the *darśanas* outlined above; it is the final component to bring into this overview. Well before the Common Era different forms of Buddhism had emerged and these generated a number of alternative forms of Buddhist philosophy. Of those that survived into the Common Era we consider some in Chapter 2, and others in Chapter 3 (where we focus on ways of thinking about the self in Indian philosophies). Not only has Buddhist philosophy had a profound impact on western thought, but – as we shall see in Chapter 6 – it was also a powerful shaping force on intellectual life in the Far East.

Nine philosophical perspectives: the *darśanas*

Āstika **– affirmers**	***Nāstika*** **– non-affirmers**
Nyāya	Cārvāka
Vaiśeṣika	Jaina
Sāṁkhya	Buddhist (taking various forms)
Yoga	
Mīmāṁsā	
Vedānta	

PHILOSOPHY AND RELIGION

As we have seen, of the nine schools or, more accurately, 'philosophical perspectives' listed in the text box, 'Nine philosophical perspectives: the *darśanas*', six are *āstika* – rooted firmly in the Vedic tradition – and the other three are *nāstika* – premised upon a decisive repudiation of the *Vedas*. Despite this disagreement, and with the exception of the Cārvākas, they all share a certain broad intellectual framework that provides a common context for their philosophical inquiries. A core element of this framework is a cyclical view of time, which may have arisen through reflection on the cycles of nature. On a cosmic level this yields the view that the world is never definitively created or destroyed, rather, over beginningless and endless aeons of time, it goes through cycles of creation, destruction and re-creation. Something similar is thought to happen to each individual human. The *darśanas* give different explanations of the details, nonetheless they share the idea that humans and other animals (and, in some versions, plants) are trapped within a repeating cycle of birth, death and rebirth. The name given to this cycle is *saṃsāra*. Another key idea which is accepted by all the *darśanas*, except Cārvāka, is that of *karma*. Again, although interpretations of the nature of *karma* differ dramatically between the *darśanas*, they share the conviction that *karma* is what holds an individual within *saṃsāra*.

This broad framework is shared by Hindus, Buddhists and Jainas; and it is more fundamental than the differences of religious affiliation or philosophical persuasion that separate them. This bedrock of shared belief, which was consolidated during the Upaniṣadic period, makes it possible to talk about all of these philosophies as part of the same family (in the same way that we can regard Jewish, Christian and Islamic philosophies as belonging to the same family because they share key ideas – such as a linear view of time and the associated notion of a Creator God). Philosophers within this family, traditionally, have not distinguished philosophical and religious questions in the way that is now common within modern western philosophy (although even there the distinction is of relatively recent provenance). Within the context provided by their shared framework of thought, philosophers in India sought to understand and explain what they took to be fundamental features of the cosmos and the nature of the individual beings within it. Asking whether their inquiries were 'religious' or 'philosophical' is to miss the point by imposing a modern distinction that does not fit the case.

On the other hand, it is undeniable that many of the philosophies of India strike western thinkers as religious. One reason for this is that, as explained above, they take for granted a certain way of looking at the world that from a modern secular perspective seems to be a religious view. The lack of defence of this view seems, to those who do not share it, to cast doubt on the legitimacy of the philosophical systems that presuppose its truth. However, if we take into account the fact that no one bothers to argue for something that everyone within a culture already accepts, it should not surprise us to find no arguments within ancient and classical Indian philosophies, for example, for the cyclical view of time or for the existence of *saṃsāra* and *karma* (McEvilley 2002).

As the philosophical systems that developed in India shared the framework of thinking briefly sketched above, they were naturally concerned with the practical quest for liberation or enlightenment – in other words, freedom from the cycle of rebirth. Many philosophers in India regarded ignorance about our true nature as the root of our entrapment in *saṃsāra*, and they believed that by liberating us from this ignorance philosophy could free us from rebirth. This explains why one of the most central concerns of philosophy in India is to arrive at a correct understanding of the self.

The attempt to reach this understanding gave rise to lively debates between people who shared enough common ground to understand each other but who were heirs to differing philosophical perspectives. As we shall see in the three chapters that follow, these debates have ranged over a number of topics that are still of interest today. But before we explore these debates, it is time to introduce another philosophical family.

PHILOSOPHY IN CHINA

Just as, because of their common origin in the cultural nexus of ancient India, and despite their differences, all the schools of philosophy in India are conventionally classified under the umbrella term 'Indian philosophy', so a number of philosophical traditions developed in China out of a common cultural nexus and – again, despite their differences – the term 'Chinese philosophy' is used to refer to them.

ORIGINS AND TEXTS

In contrast to the lands to the west with their long history of commerce and exchange of philosophical views, during antiquity the region now known as China was isolated from the rest of the world. This allowed for the emergence of a number of philosophies that were, to a remarkable degree, free of influence from ideas originating elsewhere. Thus, while philosophers in China confronted many of the same questions as did their counterparts in India and further afield, they approached these questions through the lens provided by the ancient cultures of China; and their answers were inevitably coloured by the unique perspectives provided by this lens.

Most of the philosophies that concern us in this book appeared between approximately the sixth and the end of the third century

BCE. Each was an expression and new articulation of a shared way of looking at the world that had been inherited from the past. This shared world view underwrites the claim that these otherwise diverse and sometimes adversarial philosophies are members of the same philosophical family. This section provides the background information required to understand the philosophical developments that occurred during this pivotal phase of intellectual transformation in China, developments whose legacy continues to shape East Asian cultures to this day.

Periods and dynasties up to the Qin

Neolithic cultures	
Liangzhu (Zhejiang/Jiangsu)	*c.*3300–*c.*2250 BCE*
Longshan (Shandong)	*c.*3000–*c.*1700
Xia dynasty (traditional dates are provided but the existence of this dynasty is disputed)	2205–1818
Shang dynasty	*c.*1500–*c.*1050
Zhou dynasty	
Western Zhou	*c.*1050–771
Eastern Zhou	770–221
Spring and Autumn Period	722–481
Warring States Period	403–221
Qin dynasty	221–207

*All dates are Before the Common Era.

We know a great deal about the history of the region now known as China because the textual record has been unbroken since close to the start of the first millennium BCE. This record presents us with a seamless view of China's past according to which the first dynasty, the Xia, was overthrown by the Shang dynasty, which was in turn overthrown by the Zhou (which is the point at which historical records begin). Unfortunately, it seems likely that this textual record obscures as much of the past as it reveals and so we need to appeal to non-textual sources of information to arrive at a fuller picture. While there is no independent evidence for the existence of the Xia, archaeological discoveries in the twentieth century provided a wealth of evidence for the existence and political power of the Shang. Moreover, as the archaeological record becomes more detailed it points to the existence of a diversity of contemporaneous Neolithic cultures and political entities. Just how, during the rule of the Zhou, these diverse cultures melded and assumed a recognizably 'Chinese' identity remains a mystery. Nonetheless, not only the textual record but also the evidence of material culture tells us that there was such an identity in place at the beginning of the classical era when power shifted from the Western to the Eastern Zhou (Clunas 2009). That this cultural identity was not always an entirely happy one is witnessed by the political disunity and resultant violence that characterized the later part of the rule of the Eastern Zhou; a time known – after the way it is bluntly named in the historical records of the time – as the Warring States Period. This period came to an end when the Qin dynasty assumed power in 221 BCE. Although this dynasty did not enjoy power for long it left a lasting mark due to its unification of previously independent territories. The area we now call China, with its borders that have expanded and contracted through millennia, takes its name from the Qin.

The many different philosophies that emerged during the rule of the Eastern Zhou were articulations of the culture that was consolidated during the time of the Western Zhou, a time which in retrospect was portrayed as a golden age of peace and prosperity. A fundamental concept within that culture is *Dao* (or *tao* 道), 'the way'. This concept is suggestive both of an understanding of the cosmos and of a theory about the best way to live, and it points to a vital connection between the two. The concept is firmly embedded within all the philosophies of China and, as we shall see, it underlies a consistent emphasis on continuity through change. In particular, the two main Sinitic intellectual traditions which emerged from ancient China, Confucianism and Daoism, were different interpretations of the cultural heritage that is encapsulated in the concept of *Dao*.

This cultural heritage was also transmitted by means of a text that is still well known: the *Yijing* (*I Ching*, *The Book of Changes*). Although this text reached its final form long after antiquity, important sections of it pre-date the flourishing of philosophy in China. The cosmological speculations of these early writings provided a way of understanding the world and our place within it that found a lasting place within the foundations of later Confucian and Daoist philosophies (Liu 2006: chapter 1).

PHILOSOPHICAL DEVELOPMENTS

During the time of Zhou ascendancy, society was largely agrarian and organized by a feudal system comparable to that of the European Middle Ages. However, during the Eastern Zhou this system deteriorated to such an extent that outbreaks of violence were frequent and social unrest endemic as the rulers of the various independent states engaged each other in power struggles. We can speculate that this social instability – which culminated in the Warring States Period – provoked the first attempts to think systematically about the way in which society should be organized and individuals should live. In other words, philosophy in China may have emerged as a response to these troubling social conditions. This explains the emphasis on moral and political questions found in Chinese philosophies from the earliest times through to the present day.

This book introduces the most influential forms of philosophy to emerge from this prolonged time of social unrest. In particular, it focuses on Confucian philosophies (in Chapter 4) and Daoist philosophies (in Chapter 5). Other forms of philosophy which developed in dialogue with these, such as Mohism and Legalism, are also explained. I mentioned earlier that Buddhism had a profound impact on intellectual life in China. Later (in Chapter 6) we consider a unique form of Buddhist philosophy that developed in China: namely, Chan philosophy, which climaxed during the Tang dynasty (618–906 CE). As we shall see, this involved a fusion of ideas from both India and China (when Chan later took root in Japan it became known as Zen and is now one of the most well-known forms of Buddhist philosophy in the West).

There is considerable diversity within each of the major streams of philosophy that developed in China. This diversity is not merely a feature of the way these philosophies matured through the centuries and millennia of their history; rather it can be traced back to their earliest recognizable forms and throughout their formative years. We will see that, for example, there is no such thing as 'Daoist philosophy' if what we mean by that is a set of ideas agreed upon by all Daoist thinkers. Instead certain philosophers are identified as Daoist because they have developed ideas which in retrospect seem to exemplify a Daoist approach to the world; the way in which individual thinkers flesh out these ideas, however, is idiosyncratic.

In fact, some individuals are difficult to classify as part of one philosophical tradition or another because their thought ranges over ideas that don't fit neatly into any single perspective.

Even Confucian philosophy is not composed of one fixed set of ideas. The Confucian philosophical tradition is multifaceted and has shown itself to be capable of transformation in response to new insights and changing historical circumstances. Confucian scholars have advanced a wide range of views on an equally wide range of topics and, in so doing, have on occasion arrived at some fundamental philosophical disagreements. However, all philosophers in this tradition take the *Analects*, or 'sayings', of the sage Confucius as their starting point.

Given such diversity, even within what we might casually refer to as the 'same' tradition, wherever possible we must take care to distinguish the thought of particular thinkers within the broader traditions to which they belong. We also have to remember that philosophical ideas originating geographically from China have taken root and flourished elsewhere. So a thorough study of Confucian philosophy, for example, would have to consider its manifestations outside China, particularly in Korea and Japan.

Any intellectual tradition with as long a history as that enjoyed by the ancient philosophies of China will inevitably have changed considerably through the ages. While we can't review all these changes here, we do need to be aware that we are dealing with traditions that have evolved through time. This awareness should warn us against making unhelpful generalizations about the subject. Perhaps we can take a hint from the early Chinese philosophers and bear in mind that continuity and change are partners. Through the transformations undergone by the philosophical traditions considered in this book we can see continuities that persist. As mentioned earlier, one of these continuities is the emphasis on the notion of *Dao*, the way.

PHILOSOPHY AND RELIGION

The issue of whether or not to classify Confucianism and Daoism as religions is particularly complex. While it is widely recognized that Confucianism has some characteristics that seem to be religious, such as ancestor veneration, it also has many features that do not seem to be especially religious. Part of the difficulty is that, as a product of modern western scholarship, the concept 'religion' is itself problematic and can only be applied to the traditions of China with considerable strain. Fortunately, this is not a difficulty that we need to dwell on here, as this book focuses upon specific intellectual expressions of Confucianism – Confucian philosophies. It has little to say about the practical dimensions of living one's life as a Confucian (on this see Berthrong and Berthrong 2000).

With respect to Daoism, scholars routinely distinguish between its 'religious' expression, known as *Dao-Jiao* (*Tao chiao* 道教), and its philosophical expression, which they call *Dao-Jia* (*Tao chia* 道家). Our interests in this book are on philosophical Daoism, which is the spring from which the later stream of religious Daoism flowed (for a broader introduction to Daoism, see Miller 2005).

A similar distinction can be made between Buddhism as religion and Buddhism as philosophy. Throughout the ages, many educated Chinese have taken a lively interest in Buddhist philosophies while not feeling that this committed them to adopting Buddhist religious practices.

In fact, Confucianism, Daoism, and Buddhism have not typically been regarded as mutually exclusive categories in China, either intellectually or practically. In China today, as in the past, individuals readily combine ideas and practices from all three traditions. Syncretism – this melding of ideas and practices – has always marked the relationship between these traditions, and this is one of the features that has made the history of philosophy in China so dynamic.

TERMINOLOGY AND TRANSLATIONS

Essential terminology used in this book is explained throughout the text. Many of the terms used do not have exact equivalents in English, so the original form of the word transliterated into the Roman alphabet is retained. As background to the study of the philosophies of Asia it helps to have some understanding of the languages in which they were written. This section provides key information about these languages.

SANSKRIT AND PĀLI – THE PHILOSOPHICAL LANGUAGES OF INDIA

Sanskrit is the name of the ancient Indo-European language in which most of the non-Buddhist philosophy of India was written. It was the language of scholarship in the same way that, for many years, Latin was the universally understood language of western scholars. The word 'Sanskrit' has a common verbal root with the word 'karma' (which can mean 'action'), and this suggests that the early users of this language saw a tight connection between their words and reality. They believed that their sacred language, provided that it was correctly pronounced, could make certain aspects of reality present. So, for example, correctly pronouncing the Sanskrit words of a sacrificial ritual would be effective in bringing about whatever the purpose of that ritual was. As success of ritual was dependent upon correct pronunciation, the rules of correct speech were carefully preserved by the elite class of Brahmins. The importance of the sacred language in ancient India was also reflected in the interests of later thinkers, and it explains why philosophy of language has always been a central component of many of the philosophies of India.

Despite the importance of correct pronunciation, over time vernacular forms of Sanskrit emerged. One of these is Pāli – the language of many early Buddhist texts. The two languages are both phonetic and are closely related. They use the same alphabet which has more letters than our Roman one. When Sanskrit or Pāli words are transliterated into the Roman alphabet the extra letters are represented by using diacritical marks, for example, *ṣ* or *ś* in addition to *s*. Because it is easier to read transliterated versions of Sanskrit and Pāli words if you know how to pronounce them, a pronunciation guide is provided in Appendix 3.

THE CLASSICAL LANGUAGE OF CHINA

The Chinese language has a completely different structure to that of any European or Indian language, and this makes it very difficult to translate Chinese texts (ancient or modern) into English. Many of the key early philosophical works are now available in several English translations, and a glance at these translations reveals the – sometimes extreme – differences of meaning that even responsible translators can arrive at from the same text.

The texts that concern us in this book were written in classical Chinese. Like modern Chinese, this was a non-phonetic language written in characters rather than alphabetic letters. For example, we have already met the character 道 which represents the word '*Dao*'.

There are two systems of Romanization used to translate these characters into a form usable by people who can't read them. The older system is known as the Wade-Giles, and you will find this in less recent books. The newer system is called Pinyin, and it is used in modern China to help youngsters get a first grip on the language. For guidelines to pronunciation of Pinyin, see Appendix 3. Most scholarly books published in English today use Pinyin and I follow this practice. However, to avoid confusion I also provide the Wade-Giles form in brackets the first time an important new word or name is introduced (for a translation conversion table see Liu 2006: 407–13).

TRANSLATIONS

Most of the original texts discussed in this book can be found in either *A Sourcebook in Indian Philosophy*, edited by Sarvepalli Radhakrishnan and Charles A. Moore (1989) or *Readings in Classical Chinese Philosophy*, edited by Philip J. Ivanhoe and Bryan W. Van Norden, 2nd edition (2005). Unless otherwise indicated, quotations and page references to Indian texts used in this book will be from the former and, in Chapters 4 and 5, quotations and page references to Chinese texts will be from the latter.

THE PHILOSOPHER'S DILEMMA

With characteristic precision, the philosopher Alasdair MacIntyre presents a dilemma:

> *Either* we read the philosophies of the past so as to make them relevant to our contemporary problems and enterprises, transmuting them as far as possible into what they would have been if they were part of present-day philosophy, and minimizing or ignoring or even on occasion misrepresenting that which refuses such transmutation because it is inextricably bound up with that in the past which makes it radically different from present-day philosophy; *or* instead we take great care to read them in their own terms, carefully preserving their idiosyncratic and specific character, so that they cannot emerge into the present except as a set of museum pieces.
>
> (MacIntyre 1986: 31)

Although MacIntyre wrote with ancient Greek philosophies in mind, each side of the dilemma he describes identifies a pole of current scholarship on the philosophies of Asia. On the one hand, the effort to make Asian philosophies accessible to readers who lack the training of Sinologists or Indologists runs the risk of distorting these philosophies by making them seem more familiar than they really are. On the other hand, losing ourselves in the Sinological or Indological details of the historical documents can leave us little to say about the relevance of these philosophies for today. The ideal, as MacIntyre recognized, is to strike a balance between these two approaches: to be responsible to the philosophies of the past whilst making them accessible and showing their relevance to the concerns and interests of today's readers. This book strives to achieve this balance.

WHAT HAPPENS NEXT?

Chapters 1 to 3 concentrate on the philosophies of India. Chapters 4 to 6 delve into the philosophies of China, with Chapter 6 examining later developments, focusing on neo-Confucian philosophy and Chan Buddhist philosophy. Together these chapters introduce the main perspectives found in Asian philosophies (although, as noted above, this book does not claim to be comprehensive). The brief concluding chapter addresses some of the similarities and differences between philosophy as it was understood and practised in India and in China, before considering the prospects and desirability of a global approach to philosophy.

The chapters follow a thematic rather than a historical sequence. Chapter 1 introduces the reader to the Indian philosophical tradition by looking at the ground rules for philosophical engagement that lie at its core. Understanding the debates about the nature of reason that took place in classical Indian philosophy is an essential first step to following arguments about other topics, such as the nature of reality (in Chapter 2) and the nature of persons (in Chapter 3). The material on persons provides a bridge from Hindu, Jaina and Buddhist philosophies into Chapter 4, which focuses on ethics and human nature within Confucian thought. This naturally leads to a discussion of authenticity, concentrating on Daoist approaches, in Chapter 5. Chapter 6 draws on material from all of the previous chapters as it elucidates the emergence of Chan Buddhism and neo-Confucianism from the creative fusion of ideas and arguments drawn from both India and China.

The aim of this short book is to leave the reader with a new appreciation of the philosophies of Asia and to inspire further study. To this latter end, each chapter closes with a guide to further reading and a general bibliography is provided at the end of the book.

REFERENCES AND FURTHER READING

INDIA

J. Brereton, 'The Upanishads', in William Theodore de Bary and Irene Bloom (eds), *Approaches to the Asian Classics* (New York: Columbia University Press, 1990). An excellent short introduction to Upaniṣadic thought.

Cathy Cantwell, *Buddhism: The Basics* (London: Routledge, 2010). A general introduction.

Matthew Dasti, 'Asian Philosophy', in Charles Taliaferro, Victoria S. Harrison, and Stewart Goetz (eds), *The Routledge Companion to Theism* (London and New York: Routledge, 2012), pp. 23–37.

Gavin Flood, *An Introduction to Hinduism* (Cambridge: CUP, 1996), chapter 2. One of the best introductions to Hinduism.

Sue Hamilton, *Indian Philosophy: A Very Short Introduction* (Oxford: OUP, 2001).

Richard King, *Indian Philosophy: An Introduction to Hindu and Buddhist Thought* (Edinburgh: Edinburgh University Press, 1999).

Bimal Krishna Matilal, 'On the Concept of Philosophy in India', in *Philosophy, Culture and Religion: Collected Essays* (Delhi: OUP, 2001).

Sarvepalli Radhakrishnan and Charles A. Moore (eds), *A Sourcebook in Indian Philosophy* (Princeton: Princeton University Press, 1989).

R. C. Zaehner, *Hinduism* (Oxford: OUP, 1966).

CHINA

John Berthrong and Evelyn Berthrong, *Confucianism: A Short Introduction* (Oxford: Oneworld, 2000).

Craig Clunas, *Art in China* (Oxford: OUP, 2009).

David A. Hall and Roger T. Ames, *Anticipating China: Thinking through the Narratives of Chinese and Western Culture* (Albany: SUNY, 1995). A book designed to help western students into Chinese philosophy.

Philip J. Ivanhoe and Bryan W. Van Norden (eds), *Readings in Classical Chinese Philosophy*, 2nd edition (Indianapolis: Hackett, 2005).

JeeLoo Liu, *An Introduction to Chinese Philosophy: From Ancient Philosophy to Chinese Buddhism* (Oxford: Blackwell, 2006). A contemporary introduction focusing on two key periods, 600–200 BCE and 300–900 CE.

James Miller, *Daoism: A Short Introduction* (Oxford: Oneworld, 2005).

Harold M. Tanner, *China: A History* (Indianapolis: Hackett, 2009).

OF GENERAL PHILOSOPHICAL INTEREST

Majid Fakhry, *A History of Islamic Philosophy* (New York and London: Columbia University Press, 2004).

Pierre Hadot, *Philosophy as a Way of Life* (Oxford: Blackwell, 1995).

W. Halbfass, *India and Europe* (New York: SUNY, 1988).

Victoria S. Harrison, *Religion and Modern Thought* (London: SCM, 2007).

Alasdair MacIntyre, 'The Relationship of Philosophy to Its Past', in Richard Rorty, J. B. Schneewind and Quentin Skinner (eds), *Philosophy in History: Essays on the Historiography of Philosophy* (Cambridge: CUP, 1986), pp. 31–48.

Thomas McEvilley, *The Shape of Ancient Thought* (New York: Allworth Press, 2002). A fascinating study of the relations between ancient Indian and ancient Greek thought.

Bertrand Russell, *History of Western Philosophy* (London and New York: Routledge, 2009).

Edward W. Said, *Orientalism* (Harmondsworth: Penguin, 2003).

Ludwig Wittgenstein, *Philosophical Investigations*, translated by G. E. M. Anscombe (Oxford: Blackwell, 1959).

1

REASON

This chapter introduces key issues concerning knowledge and our reasoning powers that occupied philosophers in classical India. For reasons to be explained below, questions about which sources of knowledge were acceptable and which forms of reasoning and procedures of debate reliably led to the truth were regarded as of paramount importance. The main ideas considered here were advanced by philosophers belonging to a number of both *āstika* (affirmer) and *nāstika* (non-affirmer) *darśanas*: principally, Nyāya, Cārvāka, Jaina and Madhyamaka ('Middle Way') Buddhist. Despite their differences these *darśanas* were united in the conviction that ignorance is the main problem facing all sentient beings. They also shared the belief that it is a problem requiring a philosophical solution. We begin, then, with the topic of ignorance.

IGNORANCE

In the philosophies of India ignorance is widely regarded as a principal source of suffering because it gives rise to the attachments that lead to rebirth. In their different ways, and despite important disagreements concerning what exactly it is that we are ignorant of, each *darśana* responded to the problem of ignorance. While religious traditions recommended certain ways of behaving – such as fasting and renouncing worldly goods – as a remedy for the attachments that arose from ignorance, philosophers sought to provide theoretical accounts explaining both what we are ignorant of and what we would know if we were not ignorant. Although the religious and philosophical responses to ignorance developed alongside each other and interpenetrated to a significant degree, here our focus is on the latter rather than the former.

Humans were, by and large, thought to be ignorant of the correct answers to two important questions: 'What is the fundamental nature of reality?' and 'What is the true self?'. These questions are intimately connected to each other and an answer to either one of them will imply an answer to the other. In developing their responses to these questions some *darśanas* prioritized finding an answer to the first, more encompassing, question while others, for example the Buddhist *darśanas*, prioritized the second. Those philosophers emphasizing our supposed ignorance of the nature of reality stimulated the interest in **metaphysics** that runs through most of the philosophical traditions of India. This interest, which was originally fuelled by soteriological concerns (that is, concerns about ultimate liberation from rebirth), led to the development of the rival philosophical systems previously outlined: Nyāya/Vaiśeṣika; Sāṁkhya/Yoga; Mīmāṁsā; several forms of Vedānta; several schools of Buddhism; and Jainism. All of these *darśanas* held that a correct understanding of metaphysical issues was the key to overcoming ignorance and thus of escaping the suffering attendant upon continual rebirth. However, each of them held distinctive views on the nature of the true self, its post-mortem destiny, and its relation to the ultimately real. In other words, despite agreement that knowledge will bring freedom from rebirth, there arose rival views about the human condition and what is required for liberation.

The existence of diverse and often conflicting views generated the need to discriminate between good and bad arguments. In the face of widespread disagreement about the answers to urgent questions, many held that it was inadequate merely to assert a position without providing a justification for it. Philosophers were expected to offer a proof that their view, or the view of their *darśana*, was the correct one. This expectation gave rise to serious analytical efforts to define good and bad arguments. Good arguments were thought to be ones that led to knowledge and thereby successfully dispelled ignorance; bad arguments were thought to be ones that did not. In this chapter we examine some of the issues underlying the notion of a good argument. We leave the question of what we might know by means of such arguments until later chapters. In Chapter 2 we focus on what might be learnt about the nature of reality, and in Chapter 3 we turn to knowledge of the self.

ARGUMENT

'Philosophy' comes from a Greek word meaning 'love of wisdom', and philosophers seek to acquire wisdom by replacing ignorance with knowledge through their practice of philosophy: a practice that, in classical India, was largely constituted by public debate (Ganeri 2001). Philosophical debate cannot proceed effectively unless the participants first agree on some fundamental issues governing the activity of philosophizing. At the most basic level a shared understanding of the structure of a good argument is vital, as is consensus on the rules of rational debate. Philosophers within the Nyāya *darśana*, whom I will henceforth refer to as Naiyāyikas, attended systematically to these matters. The term 'Nyāya' means 'the science of reasoning'; and Naiyāyikas were principally interested in philosophical methodology and the theory of knowledge (**epistemology**). Drawing on the work of earlier Buddhist logicians, they proposed what became the generally accepted framework for philosophical debates within and between all the schools of philosophy in India. Later in this chapter we will look more closely at the format and presuppositions of such debates. Here we focus on the Naiyāyikas' conception of the shape a philosophical argument should take.

The Naiyāyikas developed a sophisticated method of rational argument, which they then used to defend their other philosophical commitments. As outlined in the *Nyāya Sūtra* (book I, chapter I, sūtras 32–39, in *A Sourcebook in Indian Philosophy*, Radhakrishnan and Moore 1989: 362f.), arguments constructed according to this method have the following five-stage structure:

1 The premise to be established is stated.
2 The reason for the premise is given.
3 An example is provided.

4 The application of the example to the premise is explained.
5 The conclusion.

We can illustrate how the Naiyāyikas' method of argument works, using their own example of the fire on the hill (the following is adapted from King 1999: 131).

1 There is a fire on this hill (premise/statement).
2 Because there is smoke (reason).
3 Since whatever has smoke has fire, e.g. an oven (example).
4 There is smoke on this hill, which is associated with fire (application).
5 Therefore, there is a fire on this hill (conclusion).

This form of syllogistic reasoning (that is, reasoning from premises to a conclusion) is distinctive because of its appeal to an example in premise 3. The significance of this appeal to an example is that it lends weight to the otherwise unsupported general claim that 'whatever has smoke has fire'. Compare the above argument, with its appeal to an example, with the following shorter argument:

1 All smoke comes from fire.
2 There is smoke on the hill.
3 Therefore, there is a fire on the hill.

This is a purely formal argument insofar as the truth of the premises (1 and 2) guarantees the truth of the conclusion (3). To see this you need to recognize that the truth of the conclusion is guaranteed by the truth of the premises whether or not the world contains a smoking hill. *If* the premises are true, *then* the conclusion follows (this is what it means for an argument to be **valid** in western philosophical terminology). However, as it contains no support for the truth of the general claim in premise 1, its ability to deliver a genuine truth about the world is not established. Lacking support for premise 1, the argument does not provide us with any reason to agree with its conclusion that 'there is a fire on the hill'.

The shorter form of argument – developed by the ancient Greek philosopher, Aristotle – has been dominant in the western philosophical tradition. There is an ongoing debate about which type of argument is more effective for knowledge-production and whether or not the Nyāya form is in fact reducible to the Aristotelian form without losing its ability to generate significant conclusions. A key difference between the two forms of argument is that according to Aristotelian logic an argument can succeed (i.e. be valid) whether or not the premises are true, whereas a Nyāya argument can only succeed *if* the premises actually are true (and the point of the example is to establish this). (See King 1999: 131f.)

Despite its ability to deliver conclusions which purport to tell us something about the actual world without relying on an unsupported general claim, the Nyāya five-membered argument is weaker than the Aristotelian three-membered one. This is because it will always be vulnerable to the objection that the example is unreliable and so is unable to give sufficient support to the general claim. Richard King exposes the weakness in Nyāya argumentation by pointing out that by means of a Nyāya argument 'one might be led to believe that dawn has broken because one hears a cockerel crowing. But the cockerel may have been disturbed by a fox, or we may be the victim of an April Fool's joke' (King 1999: 133). We will see later that the Cārvākas exploited this weakness.

DEBATE

As mentioned above, in addition to refining a powerful form of argument, the Naiyāyikas developed a framework within which philosophical debates could proceed between parties holding opposing views. As part of this project the *Nyāya Sūtra* (V.II, in *Sourcebook*: 377–79) proposes a detailed list of things that can go wrong in the course of a debate. These can be considered as 'rules of reasoning' and if they are broken the disputant steps outside the rules of normal philosophical debate and thus disqualifies himself from the process. For example, according to sūtra 9: '"The unintelligible" is an argument, which, although repeated three times is understood neither by the audience nor by the opponent' (*The Sacred Books of the Hindus*, volume VIII: 171). So attempting to rely on an unintelligible argument will result in disqualification from the debate. Another strategy to avoid if one wants to participate in a philosophical debate is 'Evasion' – 'which arises if one stops an argument on the pretext of going away to attend another business' (sūtra 20, in ibid., p. 174). The development of the rules of reasoning was immensely important because they provided a framework within which the various *darśanas* could exchange ideas and engage in a common search for truth. But the Naiyāyikas recognized that not every intellectual engagement had this lofty goal and hence they distinguished between three types of debate: discussion (*vāda*); disputation (*jalpa*); and destructive criticism (*vitaṇḍā*). (*Nyāya Sūtra*, I.II.1–3.)

The first of these, *vāda*, is concerned with arriving at the truth through rational discussion. The aim is not simply to win the other party over to your view, but to work through the arguments together. Even if agreement cannot be reached, the debate will succeed if each party comes to a good understanding of the other's position. A successful debate is one in which both participants explain their position using the five-membered Nyāya form of argument and without breaking any of the rules of reasoning. However, as noted above, the Naiyāyikas were alert to the fact that not everyone is primarily motivated by the pursuit of truth and some individuals would rather win the argument even if that required defending a false view. *Jalpa* is the form of debate in which merely winning the argument is the goal, irrespective of where the truth lies. (In the western tradition we might think of the **sophists** as practising this form of debate.) The Naiyāyikas regarded *jalpa* as a genuine form of debate because it requires that the winner argues, without breaking the rules of reasoning, for a position. Unlike *vāda* and *jalpa*, the third kind of debate, *vitaṇḍā* (which literally means 'wrangling'), isn't really debate at all according to Nyāya standards. This is because the participants make no effort to reach an understanding of their opponent's point of view and instead merely assert their own position.

Of these three forms of engagement, *vāda* is the most important to the Naiyāyikas. It requires two main participants, a proponent who holds an initial position and a respondent; a witness or arbiter is also present. The progress of the debate can be broken down into the following steps (paraphrased from King 1999: 134f.).

1 The proponent is invited to state his thesis.
2 If the thesis is thought to be erroneous the respondent may refute it immediately, but if the thesis is accepted, then the respondent asks the proponent to outline the reason for accepting the thesis.
3 The proponent then offers a proof outlining the reasons why the thesis should be accepted.

4 The respondent asks if the proof offered contains the logical relations required of a sound inference (the Nyāya recognized five types of fallacious reasoning, see *Nyāya Sūtra*, I.II.4–9).
5 The proponent replies by 'removing the thorns', that is, he negates any faulty logical relations that may have occurred in outlining the proof of his thesis.

The debate will finish there if the respondent accepts the thesis and the proof. However, if the respondent is not convinced by the proof, a further stage of debate begins in which the respondent makes a formal statement refuting the proponent's thesis. This statement becomes the starting point for the respondent to explain the refutation in detail. It is vital that the refutation is based on the arguments used and evidence accepted by the initial proponent. The proponent is then given an opportunity to reply to the refutation if he thinks that it is mistaken. If the refutation is accepted the debate moves on to its final stage, in which the respondent formally states the refutation but this time in the form of a positive position. This positive position might then be used as the initial thesis of a new debate.

This framework for debate was developed to be conducive to the exchange and clarification of ideas. The respondent is not allowed simply to contradict the proponent's thesis and advance another in its place. Instead the thesis has to be thoroughly examined in the terms offered by the proponent. The respondent has to put himself into the mindset of the proponent and appreciate the force of the arguments from that person's point of view. The Naiyāyikas held that from this vantage point the respondent would be well-positioned to identify any logical incoherence in the proponent's defence of his thesis.

The Naiyāyikas valued *vāda* well above the two other kinds of engagement. The *Nyāya Sūtra* states: '*Jalpa* and *vitaṇḍā* are [to be employed] for protecting the ascertainment of truth, just as fences with thorny branches are constructed to protect the seedling coming out of the seed' (IV.II.50, in King 1999: 136). In other words, *jalpa* and *vitaṇḍā* can legitimately be deployed as devices to ensure that the truth prevails when an opponent is not motivated by the search for truth, and, in the case of *vitaṇḍā*, does not respect the rules of reasoning and therefore cannot be engaged in fully rational debate. But *vāda* is the key to knowledge-production and it is through this that the debating parties can expect to arrive at the truth. (For an excellent exposition of *vāda*, see King 1999: 130–37.) We have seen that the deepest purpose of rational debate was to arrive at knowledge of the truth. In the next section we consider what knowledge is.

KNOWLEDGE

Philosophers from the various *darśanas* used the framework of debate outlined above to argue with each other about many topics. Views about the nature of reality and the identity of the true self were often the subjects of such debate. But, as mentioned above, for debate about these matters to occur, all those involved had to agree to participate in a common process: in effect, acceptance of the rules of reasoning and the Nyāya method of argument became the presuppositions of rational debate. However, these were not the only requirements. If *vāda* was to provide a framework in which different philosophical views could be rationally explored and, perhaps, resolved, participants also had to agree on what counts as knowledge. In an attempt to satisfy this requirement the Naiyāyikas proposed a complex account of what knowledge is. At the core of their account was the conviction that how we come to know something is of crucial significance, and they claimed that genuine knowledge has to be produced by a reliable source. Identifying reliable sources of knowledge thus became central to the practice of philosophy in classical India.

In Sanskrit the term '*pramāna*' denotes a source of knowledge. Naiyāyikas accepted four *pramānas* (which are outlined in *Nyāya Sūtra*, I.I, in *Sourcebook*: 359): these were perception (*pratyakṣa*), inference (*anumāna*), comparison (*upamāna*) and verbal testimony (*śabda*). Unsurprisingly there was considerable controversy about the actual reliability of these proposed sources of knowledge. One reason for the persistence of this controversy was that disagreements concerning the *pramānas* could not be resolved within the framework of *vāda*. This is because to engage in *vāda* the proponent and respondent were required to share certain assumptions about which sources we can trust to yield knowledge. To see this, try to imagine a debate between a proponent who believes, for example, that perception is a reliable source of knowledge and a respondent who does not believe this. The two would not have enough common ground for the debate to get under way. The debate could only proceed if one of them agreed to suspend his convictions and accept the other's view for the duration of the debate. But then the debate couldn't succeed anyway because as soon as it was over the one who had only temporarily given up his own view could merely return to it. So agreement about which sources of knowledge are reliable is a presupposition for a successful rational debate.

At issue was the attempt to identify what might justify a claim to know something. For example, if Bimal were to assert that there is an elephant on the beach you would probably ask him how he knows this. You would expect him to give a reason for his assertion that would appeal to the way that he acquired the belief that there is an elephant on the beach. Bimal might claim to have seen the elephant, and this would be an attempt to justify his assertion on the basis of what he has perceived. Whether or not you come to accept his assertion will then crucially depend on whether or not you believe that perception is a reliable source of knowledge about such things as elephants on beaches. If you do not accept this then – provided that you are rational – you will dismiss Bimal's assertion that there is an elephant on the beach unless he can provide another reason to justify it.

While the Naiyāyikas' account of the necessity of establishing which *pramānas* were reliable was generally accepted, the various *darśanas* quibbled over the details. Perceptual experience was regarded as the least controversial of the proposed sources of knowledge. What was given to us perceptually was widely thought to be beyond dispute, so discussion between the schools focused on the reliability of the other three *pramānas*. The Naiyāyikas were alone in their support of the reliability of comparison (which we might call analogy). Their idea was that comparison could be relied upon to generate knowledge because through comparison of two known things one can infer knowledge of some third thing. For instance, if I know that both lemons and grapefruit are sour, when someone describes to me another fruit, say a lime, that seems to have some comparable properties to lemons and grapefruit, by analogy I might claim to know that limes are sour. Those in the other schools were of the view that comparison is really just a version of inference and not an independent source of knowledge in its own right.

Most of the disagreement between the *darśanas* then concerned the reliability of inference and of testimony. We briefly consider testimony here before examining inference in the following section. Knowing something on the basis of testimony at root means that you know it because someone has reported to you that it is the case. To return to the example of Bimal and the elephant, you might come to know that there is an elephant on the beach because Bimal has told you. The source of your knowledge is Bimal's testimony. It is undeniable that we rely on testimony for many of the things we claim to know. I might, for instance, know that Mumbai is a very crowded city, even though I have never been there. I might know this because of testimony that I have heard or read. The fact that testimony can come in written form gives us a clue about why it was regarded with particular interest in classical India. The *Vedas* were thought, at least by the *āstika darśanas*, to provide us with knowledge through testimony. However, some took this to be problematic because, whereas in everyday cases – such as that of Bimal's elephant – we can check the testimony if we want to, this is not so with the testimony provided by the *Vedas*. Because testimony cannot always be independently checked it was regarded as an unreliable source of knowledge by the *nāstika darśanas* (as well as by the *āstika* Vaiśeṣika).

Table 1.1 shows the stances of the various *darśanas* on the reliability of testimony and inference. The table reveals that the Cārvākas held the most radical position, rejecting both inference and testimony as reliable sources of knowledge. In the following section we turn to the Cārvākas' analysis of inferential reasoning, which played a key role

Table 1.1 Stances of the *darśanas* on the reliability of testimony and inference

School	*Inference*	*Testimony*
Nyāya	Reliable	Reliable
Vaiśeṣika	Reliable	Not reliable
Sāṁkhya	Reliable	Reliable
Yoga	Reliable	Reliable
Mīmāṁsā	Reliable	Reliable
Vedānta	Reliable	Reliable
Cārvāka	Not reliable	Not reliable
Madhyamaka Buddhist	Reliable	Not reliable
Jaina	Reliable	Not reliable

in pushing those who accepted inference to clarify and refine their position.

INFERENCE

At its most basic inference is the process of moving from acceptance of some proposition to acceptance of another. A moment's reflection reveals that we engage in this kind of reasoning process frequently in our daily lives. For example, when I perceive that my car is not in the driveway I accept the proposition that my car is absent, and from that I might infer the further proposition that my husband has gone out. This form of reasoning is so common it is hardly surprising that philosophers have taken an interest in it. Logicians and epistemologists through the centuries, and in different cultures, have attempted to classify types of inference. They have also sought to explain how inference works and to identify methods of argument that reliably capture good inferences while helping us to identify bad ones. We have already seen that the Naiyāyikas were engaged in just such an attempt.

Earlier we looked at the stock example of an inferential argument that was presented in the five-membered argumentative form developed by the Nyāya. Consider it again:

1 There is a fire on this hill.
2 Because there is smoke.
3 Since whatever has smoke has fire, e.g. an oven.
4 There is smoke on this hill, which is associated with fire.
5 Therefore, there is a fire on this hill.

As we have seen, among the *darśanas* the Cārvākas alone rejected the conclusions of inferential arguments such as this one. We now consider why they did so. We focus on the arguments of Jayarāśi, who was active in the seventh century CE. He is commonly thought to be the author of the book known as the *Tattvopaplavasiṃha* (*The Lion of Destruction of Philosophical Theories*, alternatively translated as *The Lion of Annihilation of Principles*).

The principal opponents which Jayarāśi had in view were the Naiyāyikas, although in disagreeing with them he was also disagreeing with practically everyone else. The *Tattvopaplavasiṃha* ends with the claim: 'So with [all] philosophical theories in this way leading to [their own] destruction, conventional views may be enjoyed only for as long as they remain unexamined' (in King 1999: 19). At the core of Jayarāśi's criticism of philosophical theories was his rejection of inference as a reliable source of knowledge.

Jayarāśi set out to reveal the difficulty with inferential reasoning by criticizing the Naiyāyikas attempt to establish that there is a fire on the hill by their appeal to the general premise that smoke and fire go together. (See also *Sarvadarśanasaṃgraha*, in *Sourcebook*: 230–31.) He claimed that, far from constituting knowledge, conclusions reached by inferential arguments such as this one were nothing but products of the imagination lacking rational foundations. This is because, as we have seen, they depend on a general premise (usually containing words like 'all' or 'wherever'). Jayarāśi pointed out that citing an example, such as the oven, could never be sufficient to establish general claims that would be true about all times and in all cases. (And we might reflect that nowadays we are familiar with instances of smoke that are not associated with fire, when the smoke is caused by dry ice during theatrical performances for instance.) By criticizing inference in this way, Jayarāśi discovered what is now known to western philosophers as the problem of **induction**. This problem was brought to light in the West by David Hume (1771–76) and subsequently assumed a central place within western philosophy.

To see the problem consider how you would try to defend a claim such as 'wherever there is smoke there is fire'. You might try to enumerate instances of smoke you had experienced that were accompanied by an experience of fire and then draw the general conclusion that smoke is always attended by fire. In other words you would rely on an inductive argument like this one:

1 One year ago I had an experience of smoke that was attended by fire.
2 Last week I had an experience of smoke that was attended by fire.
3 Yesterday I had an experience of smoke that was attended by fire.
4 Today I had an experience of smoke that was attended by fire.
5 Therefore, wherever there is smoke there is fire.

Jayarāśi argued that such inductive arguments can never guarantee the truth of their conclusions. The core problem is that while premises like 1 to 4 rely on our experience, our experience could never enable us to be sure that any conclusion such as 5 was true. In other words, our past and present experiences could never tell us that in all cases smoke was attended by fire; they could only tell us that this was the case in the finite number of instances of fire we had witnessed. Specifically, our experience could not tell us anything about whether smoke in the past which we hadn't witnessed was attended by fire, or whether smoke in the future that we are not currently in a position to witness will be so attended (see *Sourcebook*: 231).

Jayarāśi seems to have identified a real problem at the heart of our practice of inductive inference. One possible response to this problem is to claim that the practice must be legitimate because it is so remarkably successful. Given that most of our scientific knowledge is based on induction, its success seems undeniable. However, Jayarāśi argued in response that this pragmatic defence of induction is inadmissible because it relies on induction! Thus it involves a circular argument (a point also made by Hume). We would have to appeal to a generalization based on our past experience of apparently successful induction (this is evident in the argument set out above). But this reasoning process would itself be an example of inductive inference, as we would have to infer that the future will be like the past.

CAUSATION

Another strategy to defend inference would be to provide a convincing account of why it is that inferential reasoning often leads us to accept conclusions that turn out to be true, a fact which would seem to validate this way of reasoning. In other words, we might seek an explanation of the apparent success of induction. Early Cārvākas attempted to block this manoeuvre with their claim that the success of such reasoning is nothing more than a happy accident. If in some instance an inference appears to be vindicated this is the result of an accident rather than anything intrinsic to the reasoning process (see *Sourcebook*: 233). But this claim seems to be inadequate because it does not actually explain anything. It might seem more plausible to look for an underlying connection between the two things connected by the inference. One proposal is that inference works because it tracks the causal relationship between two things, such as fire (the cause) and smoke (the effect). It is the causal relationship between fire and smoke which leads us to believe that all cases of smoke will be caused by fire; and this relationship is what underwrites our conclusion that any particular instance of smoke must be caused by fire.

> We often infer the existence of a particular cause from the existence of a particular effect. This is what happens, for example, when we see an elephant's footprint in the sand (let that be our effect) and we infer that there is (or has recently been) an elephant on the beach (that will be our cause). Inference allows us to draw conclusions about an unseen cause on the basis of an observed effect. Most people regard this practice as a reliable way to acquire knowledge about the world. Cārvākas argued that they are mistaken to do so.

Jayarāśi realized that our beliefs about causation often lend plausibility to our inferences, and so many of the arguments in the *Tattvopaplavasiṃha* attempt to undermine our confidence in the notion of causation. One argument aims 'to refute inference based on the effect' (*Sourcebook*: 239). Jayarāśi seeks to convince us that there is no such thing as causation by proving that there are no effects. His argument assumes that effects begin and end at some point in time. The reason for this assumption is the not-implausible claim that if a purported effect existed perpetually it would not in fact be an effect. Jayarāśi argues that for something, for example, a footprint, to be identified as an effect we must directly perceive it ceasing to exist; but we can never directly perceive anything ceasing to exist, because if it has ceased to exist we could not perceive it at all. Things either exist, and can be directly perceived, or don't exist, and cannot be directly perceived. So we cannot establish that anything is an effect, thus our notion of causation appears to be redundant.

Jayarāśi puts forwards another argument that seeks to demonstrate 'the impossibility of understanding the relation of cause and effect' (*Sourcebook*: 242–46). Here he claims that the supposed relation between causes and their effects is unintelligible; therefore it cannot be used to legitimize the process of inferential reasoning. His main argument for this claim is that understanding the relation between a cause and its supposed effect demands that we perceive (that is, experience) the cause independently of its relation to the supposed effect. But if we can only perceive the cause as the cause of the effect, then we can never know it independently. The cause-and-effect relation itself makes knowledge of the cause unqualified by the effect impossible. Another way of putting this is to say that a cause is only a cause once it has caused an effect. If it is not a cause before the production of the effect, it cannot be known as a cause before the production of the effect. If it cannot be known as a cause before the production of the effect, it can only be known when it is qualified by the effect. Thus we can never have knowledge of a cause which is unqualified by the effect.

On the basis of such arguments, Jayarāśi holds that we are not justified in accepting the conclusions of inferential arguments on the basis of a posited causal relationship that they successfully track. And, as we saw above, nor does he believe that our inferential practices are vindicated by our experience. He concludes that our practice of inference is entirely unsupported. This is a very serious assertion given the centrality of inferential reasoning to most of what we normally claim to know about the world. If we accept Jayarāśi's arguments we should be sceptical about all claims that are not grounded directly in our experience. However, notice that in order to present his own arguments Jayarāśi has been forced to employ inference. To follow his 'proof' that there is no such thing as causation, for example, requires accepting a complex chain of inferences from one proposition to another. In effect, he has demonstrated the extent to which we rely on inference if we want to defend any position at all – even a sceptical one!

The arguments about causation reviewed above also reveal the extent to which, despite his scepticism about causation, Jayarāśi was committed to the reliability of perception as a source of knowledge. In the following section we are introduced to a Buddhist philosopher who is sceptical even about perception.

SCEPTICISM

The Cārvākas were not alone in subjecting the Naiyāyikas' theory of knowledge to searching philosophical criticism. Nāgārjuna (second century CE), who was foundational to the Buddhist Madhyamaka tradition, was another influential critic of Nyāya thought. His main criticism was that the Naiyāyikas think that by establishing what the sources of knowledge are they have thereby established that the objects of knowledge (*prameyas*) exist; and that by establishing that the objects of knowledge exist they have thereby established that the sources of knowledge are reliable (because the sources of knowledge allow us to know the objects). Nāgārjuna elegantly argues that this circular reasoning can prove neither that the purported objects of knowledge exist nor that the purported sources of knowledge are reliable (see *Vigrahavyāvartani*, 46–49, in King 1999: 138).

Presuming agreement on the acceptable sources of knowledge, the Naiyāyikas believed that they had also secured agreement that the objects of knowledge really existed. Knowing that there is an elephant on the beach through a reliable source such as perception seemed to them to entail that the elephant on the beach really existed independently of the fact that anyone knew it was there. They held what is known today as a theory of naïve – or direct – **realism** about the existence of the objects that make up the world. Their difficulty was to defend this view without resorting to the circular strategy of appealing to the way things actually appear to us. In other words the key assumption is that the objects in the world exist independently of our minds. But the problem that must be surmounted in order to defend this assumption is that we never have access to these purported objects independently of the way that they appear to us, so we could never be in a position to compare the actual objects with our perceptions of them. There seems to be nothing to stop a critic, such as Nāgārjuna, arguing that appearances are an illusion generated by the mind.

In response to such criticisms of the reliability of the sources of knowledge, some Naiyāyikas argued that the *pramānas* were self-evidently reliable; their reliability could not be doubted, as they were given along with the object of knowledge. We have already seen how Nāgārjuna responded to that suggestion. He also pointed out the further problem that the Naiyāyikas' view doesn't take seriously cases in which we are led to hold false beliefs by the *pramānas*. Inferences often lead us to false conclusions (for example, the reason why my car is absent from the driveway might be that it has been stolen, not that my husband has gone out). Moreover, there do seem to be genuine cases of perceptual illusion. Within western philosophy the stick which appears bent under water is a favourite example;

Indian philosophers preferred the example of the coil of rope that looks like a snake in the dim light of dusk. Another problem with the claim that the *pramānas* are self-evidently reliable is that philosophers like Nāgārjuna could retort 'well, we manage to doubt these things'.

In the face of such problems, Naiyāyikas tried a different kind of defence of their view that the *pramānas* were reliable. They argued that the traditionally accepted *pramānas* were to be trusted on the grounds that they allowed us to plan actions and carry them through successfully. This is a pragmatic argument which appeals to the practical success of the accepted sources of knowledge. We have already seen how Cārvākas replied to this argument, and the same response is available to Nāgārjuna: the apparent success of the *pramānas* might be nothing more that a happy accident. Nāgārjuna in fact replied with the incisive observation that in attempting to justify their faith that the *pramānas* are reliable, the Naiyāyikas are giving up the idea that the *pramānas* are the ultimate court of appeal for knowledge claims. Once you start along the road of justifying the *pramānas*, he noted, you are on the way to a potentially infinite regress.

We have seen that each one of the purported sources of knowledge can be criticized, and none of them – even perception – is so uncontroversial that it is universally accepted. Given this unfortunate situation, Nāgārjuna proposed that we should refrain from claiming to know anything. Because he regarded each of the sources of knowledge accepted by the Naiyāyikas as unreliable, he was also convinced that the framework of debate they advocated was pointless. He argued that if what we take to be the most basic justifications for our claims to know anything are demonstrably unreliable, then the edifice of debate founded upon them could not be legitimate either. This is what motivated his famous declaration: 'If I were to put forward any thesis whatsoever, then by that I would have made a logical error. But I do not put forward a thesis. Therefore I am not in error' (*Vigrahavyāvartani*, 29, in King 1999: 138).

In attempting to defend their position against those such as Nāgārjuna and the Cārvākas the Naiyāyikas were confronted with the problem of **scepticism** which afflicts every philosophy, both ancient and modern. Philosophers have been puzzling over sceptical challenges to our claims to know anything – even that we ourselves exist – for as long as philosophy has been practised. The sceptics were as much a thorn in the side of the Naiyāyikas as they were to modern philosophers in the western tradition, such as René Descartes. In the remainder of this chapter we turn to another attempt to deal with the problem of scepticism, one which sought to integrate a plurality of perspectives.

PERSPECTIVES

If the philosophical tools developed by the Naiyāyikas are insufficient to allow rational people to reach agreement about important philosophical questions, might another approach fare any better? To answer this question we turn to another *nāstika darśana* that grappled with this issue.

Jainism became a recognizable tradition in India at about the same time as Buddhism did, although Jaina teachings have a much longer history than this fact suggests (McEvilley 2002). Despite this more ancient heritage, tradition regards Māhavīra (599–527 BCE) as the founder of Jainism. Jaina philosophy has distinctive views on many of the topics covered by classical Indian philosophy and it concerns us here because it advances a theory that, if successful, reconciles many of the core insights embedded within the apparently conflicting philosophical views advanced by the rival *darśanas*.

Jainas hold that reality is many-sided (*anekānta*) and that people adopt different perspectives (*nayas*) which allow them to see selective aspects of reality. But by doing this they can never see the whole because any one perspective is only capable of giving them partial knowledge of an object. This conviction led Jainas to claim that any single assertion about a thing will be incapable of expressing the whole nature of that thing. Therefore, our assertions about things cannot be unconditionally true, but only true in a certain respect.

Consider this example from a Jaina text, the *Sanmati Tarka*, which illustrates two perspectives on the question of whether things are subject to birth and decay (i.e. change) or whether they possess something stable (such as a permanent substance):

> These three characteristics of birth, decay and stability must dwell together in harmony to make a real definition of a thing in its integral form. Each *naya* [perspective], therefore, if taken independently, isolated from the other, can never yield an adequate idea of an entity. Both these therefore, divorced from each other, are wrong in their standpoints.

> As these two *nayas* when taken in their exclusiveness are false *nayas*, all other *nayas* also are wrong when taken in their isolated standpoints, for the subsequent *nayas* occupy themselves in viewing the different aspects of the thing which is the subject of these two principal *nayas*.
> (*Sourcebook*: 269)

The first perspective – that things are subject to birth and decay – is the Buddhist view (which we consider in Chapter 3); the second perspective – that things possess an underlying stability – is the Vaiśeṣika view. Both perspectives, according to the Jaina, contain some truth. On the one hand, all things change, on the other hand, change could not take place unless there was a stable underlying thing that was changing. The problem with non-Jaina philosophers, then, is that they settle upon one perspective and argue that it is exclusively correct. In so doing, they reach false conclusions because the truth available through any single perspective is only a partial truth. To arrive at the full truth different perspectives must be combined, as all serious metaphysical positions contain a core of truth – even ones that appear to be diametrically opposed.

LOGIC

The example considered above seems to entail that a single object can be the bearer of contradictory properties (in this case, stability and change) and this suggests that the Jaina are committed to asserting contradictions. However, this is far from being the case as they regarded the presence of a contradiction to be a fault in a theory and they believed that they had found a way to avoid this fault.

The Jaina believed that one could assert such claims as '*A* has property *f*' and '*A* does not have property *f*' without contradicting oneself. They argued that in our experience we routinely come across instances of objects both possessing and not possessing a particular property. In such a case, we will not hold that our experience is contradictory so we should not hold that the assertions we form on the basis of our experience are contradictory. Consider, for example, a cloth with two colours, blue and grey. What colour is this cloth? A Buddhist answer would be that the cloth has no colour at all and only the individual threads have colour – some being blue and others being grey. The Vaiśeṣika, on the other hand, would answer that the cloth has a single new colour – call it bley – which is the product of a mixture of the colours of its parts. Both of these views are extremes and, according to Jaina thinking, both are contrary to common sense. The Jaina position is that the cloth is both blue and not blue, and both grey and not grey. As we have seen, their claim is that properties such as 'blue' and 'not blue' are not contradictory because we regularly encounter them in our experience and our experience is not contradictory. The Jainas advanced a theory of language to explain how we can say both that 'the cloth is blue' and that 'the cloth is not blue' without actually contradicting ourselves.

To see what they proposed, think about the statement 'tomorrow I am going to fast'. If I utter this now, you will understand that *tomorrow* I am going to fast. However, if you come across an undated note with 'tomorrow I am going to fast' written on it you will have no idea which day 'tomorrow' refers to. This is because, as the Jaina would say, there are hidden parameters governing the use of the word 'tomorrow'. In the example, there is no explicit difference between the two phrases, the one spoken and the one written, but there is nonetheless an implicit difference. Jainas hold that all of our assertions have hidden parameters like this and that, because they are not made clear, the way we normally use language is vague. They claim that when the language we use is made specific by spelling out the parameters we will see that there might be no contradiction involved in assertions of the form '*Fa*' and 'not *Fa*' – or, for instance, 'blue' and 'not blue'.

Jainas have rejected the widely accepted principle that assertion and denial are mutually exclusive alternatives. In their view, assertion does not rule out denial because of the hidden parameters governing the scope of particular assertions and denials. With respect to one set of parameters, one might be able to assert '*X*', while, with respect to another set, one might be able to assert 'not *X*'. They attempt to explain this further by means of their theory of seven modes (*saptabhaṅgī*), according to which any statement can be asserted in seven possible ways. The seven modes of assertion are illustrated below using the example of an object that may be blue:

1 asserting that the object is blue;
2 denying that the object is blue;

3 assert–denying that the object is blue (i.e. claiming that according to one set of parameters the object is blue, while according to another set it is not blue);
4 both asserting and denying that the object is blue;
5 both asserting and assert–denying that the object is blue (with different values for the hidden parameters);
6 both denying and assert–denying that the object is blue (with different values for the hidden parameters);
7 asserting, denying and assert–denying that the object is blue (with different values for the hidden parameters). (See Ganeri 2001: 138)

Jainas claim that these seven modes are to be understood as qualified by the term 'somehow' (*syāt*). To see this take the statement 'the object is blue' and render it 'somehow the object is blue'. 'Somehow' ranges over the parameters of substance, time, place and state. How this device works is demonstrated by Malliṣeṇa, a twelfth-century Jaina philosopher. He is answering the question 'does the pot exist?':

> '*syāt*' – somehow, through its own substance, place, time and state, the pot and all indeed exists, not through another substance, place, time and state. So a pot exists as regards substance by being made of earth, but not by being made of water. As regards place, [it exists] by being in Pāliputra, not by being in Kānyakubja. As regards time, [it exists] by being in the winter, not by being in the spring. As regards state, [it exists] by being black, not by being red.
>
> (In Ganeri 2001: 139)

Now consider again the assertion that 'the object is blue'. Clearly, it will have to be evaluated in terms of each of the parameters. The mere claim that 'the object is blue' is, as it stands, neither true nor false because it is underspecific. Only assertions that have their hidden parameters made explicit can be evaluated for truth or falsity. So the statement 'the object is blue' has to be transformed into 'with respect to some substance, place, time and state the object is blue'. Once the statement is put into this form, it is clear that 'the object is blue' could be correctly asserted with respect to some of the parameters but not to others. For example, it could be correctly asserted that 'the object is blue' with respect to this time, place and state but incorrectly asserted with respect to another time, place and state. The object may have been recently dyed a different colour or sold to someone in a different region.

Let us now see how an analysis of the claim that 'the object is blue' might proceed according to the theory of seven modes of assertion (here I follow Ganeri 2001). To (1) assert that the object is blue is to claim that there is a set of parameters according to which the object is blue. But this does not rule out (2) denying that the object is blue, because this is to claim that there is a set of parameters according to which the object is not blue. So (1) and (2) are not contradictory. What about (3), assert–denying that the object is blue? This is to claim that there is a set of parameters according to which the object is blue and a set of parameters according to which the object is not blue. The point is to show that it is possible to assert that the object is blue, deny that the object is blue, and to assert and deny that the object is blue. Each possibility involves a different mode of talking about the object.

Now consider (4), both asserting and denying that the object is blue. The claim cannot be that according to some set of parameters the object is blue and is not blue. That would be a genuine contradiction. Instead, 'somehow' functions in this mode of assertion as an expression of ignorance. It is to say 'either the object is blue or the object is not blue, but I don't know which'. This mode of assertion will be used when knowledge about an object is deficient in the sense that we don't know the relevant parameters.

From the possibility of the first four modes of assertion, the possibility of the other three follows. It then emerges that it is possible to make all seven kinds of assertion about the same object with respect to the same property.

Jainas contrast statements qualified by 'somehow' with statements made from a particular perspective. This is because they believed that a complete description of an object is possible if we take into account all possible modes of assertion and hence all relevant parameters. A complete description of an object just is a description that ranges over all the parameters and employs all relevant modes of assertion. Essentially, the Jainas claim that complete knowledge of an object is available through applying the theory of seven modes; whereas only partial knowledge is available through adopting a perspective.

With their theory of seven modes and their account of the limited nature of perspectives, the Jainas proposed a novel framework within which to think about the rival philosophical commitments of the various *darśanas*. As we shall see in the following two chapters, the conceptual generosity of their proposal did nothing to quell the debates that were the lifeblood of philosophy in classical India.

SUMMARY OF CHAPTER 1

This chapter has explored the key methods and epistemological concepts used in the philosophies of India. It began with a section on ignorance because this is the core problem confronting philosophical and religious thinkers, whether Hindu, Buddhist or Jaina. If ignorance is the core problem, then the solution is knowledge. But how can we come to knowledge? In one way or another, this question pre-occupied philosophers in India irrespective of their school. Moreover, the philosophers within each school did not arrive at their views independently, but in debate with those from other schools. For this to be possible they had to agree about what was to count as rational argumentation. Philosophers from the various schools also argued about what could justify knowledge-claims. Debates between the Nyāya, the Cārvākas and the Buddhist Madhyamaka school about this issue were examined.

The chapter closed with a discussion of Jaina views. Jainas confronted the same epistemological problems as members of the other *darśanas*. However, they sought to accommodate the diverse viewpoints available within a pluralist logical system designed to explain how apparently conflicting perspectives could each make a contribution to our grasp of the truth. Their logical system was thus a direct response to the philosophical disagreements explained in this chapter.

The focus on the theory of knowledge in this chapter provides a platform into the discussion of metaphysics in the following chapter – where we consider different theories about the fundamental nature of reality.

REFERENCES AND FURTHER READING

PRIMARY TEXTS

Nyāya Sūtra (associated with Akṣapāda Gotama *c.*250–450 CE). The foundational text of the Nyāya school. In *Sourcebook*, pp. 358–79. Also in volume VIII of *The Sacred Books of the Hindus* (New York: AMS Press, 1974).

Siddhasena Divākara, *Sanmati Tarka*. In *Sourcebook*, pp. 269–71. A text outlining the Jaina view on perspectives.

Jayarāśi, *Tattvopaplavasiṃha*. Arguably an authentic Cārvāka text from the seventh century CE. In *Sourcebook*, pp. 236–46.

Mādhavācārya, *Sarvadarśanasaṃgraha*, edited and translated by Madan Mohan Agarwal (Delhi: Chaukambha Sanskrit Pratishthan, 2002). An explanation and critique of key aspects of Cārvāka.

Sarvepalli Radhakrishnan and Charles A. Moore (eds), *A Sourcebook in Indian Philosophy* (Princeton: Princeton University Press, 1989).

SECONDARY LITERATURE

Piotr Balcerowicz, *Jaina Epistemology in Historical and Comparative Perspective* (Wiesbaden: Franz Steiner, 2000).

G. Chemparathy, *An Indian Rational Theology: Introduction to Udayana's Nyāyakusumānjali* (Vienna: Gerold & Co, 1972).

Eli Franco, *Perception, Knowledge and Disbelief: A Study of Jayarāśi's Scepticism* (Delhi: Motilal Banarsidass, 1994).

Jonardon Ganeri, *Philosophy in Classical India: The Proper Work of Reason* (London: Routledge, 2001).

Padmanabh S. Jaini, *The Jaina Path of Purification* (Berkeley: University of California Press, 1979).

Richard King, *Indian Philosophy: An Introduction to Hindu and Buddhist Thought* (Edinburgh: Edinburgh University Press, 1999). Chapter 6 introduces the *pramānas*. For Nāgārjuna's critique of *pramāna-vāda*, see pp. 137–45.

Thomas McEvilley, *The Shape of Ancient Thought* (New York: Allworth Press, 2002).

Bimal Krishna Matilal, *Epistemology, Logic and Grammar in Indian Philosophical Analysis* (Oxford: OUP, 2005).

Bimal Krishna Matilal, *Perception: An Essay on Classical Indian Theories of Knowledge* (Oxford: Clarendon Press, 1986).

Jitendra Nath Mohanty, *Reason and Tradition in Indian Thought* (Oxford: Clarendon Press, 1992).

Y. J. Padmarajiah, *Jaina Theories of Reality and Knowledge* (Bombay: Jain Sahitya Vikas Mandal, 1963).

Stephen Phillips, *Classical Indian Metaphysics: Refutations of Realism and the Emergence of 'New Logic'* (Chicago: Open Court, 1995).

Karl Potter (ed.), *Encyclopedia of Indian Philosophies*, volume 2. *Nyāya-Vaisesika* (Delhi: Motilal Banarsidass, 1977).

2

REALITY

Two questions preoccupied philosophers in classical India; as explained in the previous chapter, these questions concerned, firstly, the nature of reality and, secondly, the identity of the true self. Here we explore some answers to the first question and in the following chapter we focus on answers to the second.

Philosophers proposed and defended a number of competing accounts of the nature of reality. Some argued for a pluralist account, according to which reality is composed of an irreducible plurality of different types of object. Others preferred the dualist thesis that reality is composed of two fundamentally different substances. A third type of theory, called **monism**, held that, despite appearances to the contrary, at the most fundamental level only one thing was real. Supporters of each position held that their account was faithful to the *Vedas*. A key subject of debate, then, was whether pluralism, **dualism** or monism offered the best theory of the fundamental nature of reality. As we shall see, seeking to resolve this debate led to extensive examination of a further question: 'What, if anything, are we directly aware of through experience?'.

Philosophers from all the *darśanas* contributed to the discussion of these questions. Here we focus on those *darśanas* which advanced the most distinctive views about the nature of reality. These are the four *āstika darśanas*, Advaita Vedānta, Sāṁkhya, Yoga and Vaiśeṣika. We will also consider some Buddhist responses to these views. We begin with a brief discussion of pre-philosophical speculation about the origin of the world (and of selves) in the *Vedas*.

ORIGINS

As we have seen, the *Ṛg Veda* is the most ancient text we have from the Vedic Period (some portions of it are from *c.*1500 BCE). It contains the earliest known speculations in the literature of India about the origin of the universe. Here is the most well-known example:

> Then neither Being nor Not-being was,
> Nor atmosphere, nor firmament, nor what is beyond. ...
> That One breathed, windless, by its own energy (*svadhā*):
> Nought else existed then.
> In the beginning was darkness swathed in darkness;
> All this was but unmanifested water.
> Whatever was, that One, coming into being,
> Hidden by the Void,
> Was generated by the power of heat (*tapas*).
> In the beginning this [One] evolved,
> Became desire, first seed of mind.
> Wise seers, searching within their hearts,
> Found the bond of Being in Not-being.
> (*Ṛg Veda* 10.129.1–4, in Zaehner 1966: 11–12;
> see *Sourcebook*: 23)

In another famous passage, *Ṛg Veda* 10.90, the world is described as originating from the sacrifice of a God-like being named *Puruṣa* (*Sourcebook*: 19f.). At the core of this myth is the image of a primal cosmic person (the *Puruṣa*) being pulled apart to generate all that now exists. The myth has been very influential as it contains a rationalization of the class system that was established during the Vedic Period. The myth was probably used in the attempt to justify and explain this social structure. It tells us that hierarchical, hereditary social groups are not creations of the dominant and controlling class of society, but are instead part of the structure of the cosmos. In other words, the way that society is ordered is a reflection of the order of the cosmos. Specifically, it claims that the four classes were derived from the mouth (*brahmin*), arms (*kṣatriya*), thighs (*vaiśya*) and feet (*śūdra*) of the *Puruṣa*. The caste system was a later development of this class hierarchy.

As well as being influential on the social world, this creation myth had a significant impact on later philosophical traditions. Notice that in the myth the universe is said to be created out of one thing – the *Puruṣa* – which is pulled apart; it is easy to see how this might have led to philosophical monism: that is, the view that at the most fundamental level the universe is reducible to one thing. As we shall see later, the term '*puruṣa*' plays an important role in the Sāṁkhya *darśana* where it denotes pure consciousness. The term's meaning was transformed and the anthropomorphic dimensions of the ancient myth discarded although the idea of a primordial substance remains.

The early *Upaniṣads* mark a transitional phase away from the ancient Vedic sacrificial religion to a religion which was more concerned with the inner life. Whereas the earlier Vedic tradition emphasized correct physical or verbal performance of certain acts as sufficient for accomplishing the purpose of the rituals and sacrifices, the *Upaniṣads* claimed that knowledge is more important than performing the acts in ignorance of their real significance. The *Upaniṣads* advanced the idea that the purpose of the Vedic rituals can be accomplished within a person's mind and body without the need actually to light fires and sacrifice animals and so on.

There are over 200 *Upaniṣads*, although ten are considered to be particularly important: *Īśā*, *Kena*, *Kaṭha*, *Praśna*, *Muṇḍaka*, *Māṇḍūkya*, *Taittirīya*, *Aitareya*, *Chāndogya* and *Bṛhadāraṇyaka* (these last two are the oldest, dating from sometime before the fifth century BCE).

The *Upaniṣads* are more philosophical than any other texts within the genre of Indian sacred literature. In them we see abstract speculation emerging from the primarily mythical ideas of the earlier Vedic Period. It is not surprising then to find that the *Upaniṣads* have been more influential in the development of the schools of philosophy than have any other texts from the sacred literature. However, it would be a mistake to read the *Upaniṣads* looking for a systematic and developed philosophical or religious system. Instead of a systematic philosophy they offer key themes and teachings which were used by later philosophers as the raw material to construct the elaborate philosophical systems of the *darśanas*.

The *Upaniṣads* continued the tradition of cosmological speculation begun in the *Ṛg Veda*. The two most important themes in the *Upaniṣads* are the nature of the ultimately real (Brahman) and the identity of the true self (ātman). It is in the *Upaniṣads* that the term 'Brahman' takes on the meaning of ultimate reality. In earlier texts 'Brahman' referred to the power inherent in the Vedic ritual. By the time of the *Upaniṣads*, the term had come to denote an abstract principle: the essence of reality or the ultimately real. The point is emphasized that Brahman cannot be identified with anything in the world of our experience, such as breath or speech, as had been suggested in the earlier Vedic tradition. Instead Brahman was seen as a more fundamental reality supporting all worldly phenomena. This new, abstract use of the term 'Brahman' had momentous significance for the various philosophies that developed after this point.

A radically new understanding of the nature of reality is being introduced in the *Upaniṣads*. To help people understand this new idea various stories and images are used to explain it. The most famous is the following, found in the *Chāndogya Upaniṣad*, in which Uddalāka Āruṇi instructs his son Śvetaketu:

> 'Put this chunk of salt in a container of water and come back tomorrow.' The son did as he was told, and the father said to him: 'The chunk of salt you put in the water last evening – bring it here.' He groped for it but could not find it, as it had dissolved completely.
>
> 'Now, take a sip from this corner,' said the father. 'How does it taste?'
>
> 'Salty.'
>
> 'Take a sip from the center. – How does it taste?'
>
> 'Salty.'
>
> 'Take a sip from that corner. – How does it taste?'
>
> 'Salty.'
>
> 'Throw it out and come back later.' He did as he was told and found that the salt was always there. The father told him: 'You, of course, did not see it there, son; yet it was always right there.'
>
> (6.13.1–2, in Olivelle 1998: 255; see *Sourcebook*: 69f.)

The message is that Brahman (the ultimately real) permeates all things although it is not identified with those things (just as the salt permeates the water but is not the water). Despite Brahman's ubiquitous nature, it cannot be grasped, touched, collected or seen.

Nonetheless, the claim is that it can be experienced in some way; the next verse tells us why this might be so: 'The finest essence here – that constitutes the self of this whole world; that is the truth; that is the self (*ātman*). And that's how you are, Śvetaketu' (6.13.3, in Olivelle 1998). Brahman, the essence of the whole world, is then identified with ātman – the essence of each person. On the basis of this interpretation, different teachings developed with the aim of helping people to get beyond their experience of the everyday world in order to experience ātman and, ultimately, Brahman.

Many believed that ultimate reality could be experienced through concentrating attention on one's mental and physical states. Another way of putting this is to say that inside each person there is an entire universe to be explored. This theory has to be understood in the context of the *Puruṣa* myth which, as we saw above, taught that everything in the universe was derived from one original cosmic being. This myth established a link between the individual and the cosmic that was to persist throughout the main streams of philosophy in India. Given this understanding, it is not surprising that an expansive literature developed which purported to map this universe, to aid one in one's personal explorations. Under the influence of the *Upaniṣads*, knowledge of internal reality, which was thought to be identical to the deep reality of the universe, came to be regarded by many as the supreme aim of the ancient Vedic rituals and sacrificial tradition.

This monistic, interior knowledge-centred strand of the *Upaniṣads* is clearly in tension with the earlier Vedic tradition with its emphasis on external acts. The earlier tradition took the plurality of reality very seriously, holding that the world of our experience was real, not just an appearance hiding a deeper unitary reality. The *Upaniṣads*, in contrast, suggest that empirical 'reality' – that is, the reality which we routinely experience – is only conventionally real, although they do not come out into open confrontation with the older view. They don't, for example, suggest that the old ritual practices should be completely given up – they merely imply that they ought to be internalized.

The *Upaniṣads* also promoted the idea that the realization that ātman is Brahman is not principally an intellectual realization. It is described as an experience of joy or bliss which cannot be arrived at through logical processes of reasoning. To help in the attainment of this experience, it was commonly thought that some form of asceticism was essential. This conviction fuelled some of the stranger aspects of Indian religious culture. For example, people making vows not to sit or lie down for a number of years; or to keep an arm above one's head for the rest of one's life. Less eccentrically, the tradition of fasting is also supposed to make one more susceptible to the desired blissful realization.

The term 'yoga' comes from a Sanskrit verbal root (*yuj*) which means 'to control', 'to yoke' or 'to unite'. It is used in the *Upaniṣads* to refer to various techniques for attaining the realization that ātman and Brahman are one. Ancient sages taught that through practising yoga it is possible to transcend one's everyday experience of oneself and ultimately experience the self's genuine identity. As we shall see later, yoga is much more than a system of physical exercises; it includes a variety of ascetic practices as well as the more specific practice of meditation.

Although various yoga traditions are traceable back to the *Upaniṣads* (see especially *Bṛhadāraṇyaka Upaniṣad* 4.4.23 and *Kaṭha Upaniṣad*), which, as we have seen, are overwhelmingly monist, it wasn't long before yoga became associated with dualism rather than monism. Yoga traditions portray the self as somehow trapped within the body and the material world, and they offer techniques by means of which the real self may become disentangled from the realm of matter. This is clearly not a monist way of conceptualizing reality. As we have seen, monism claims that fundamentally only one thing exists, while dualism claims that fundamentally two things exist. The Sāṁkhya *darśana* developed a dualist metaphysical position, and it was to this that the yoga traditions quickly aligned themselves. We examine this dualist view later in the chapter.

Considering the Vedic literature as a whole for a moment, we can see that there are two very different basic understandings of reality at work within it. First, the older view which regards the empirical world of our experience as real; and second, the new monist view of the *Upaniṣads* which regards the empirical world as less than fully real and only Brahman–ātman as ultimately real. Both of these ways of conceptualizing reality were carried over into the later philosophical tradition, some *darśanas* (such as the Mīmāṁsā and the Nyāya-Vaiśeṣika pair) developing the older pluralist understanding of reality, whereas monism was championed by Vedāntins. The dualism of other *darśanas* (such as the Sāṁkhya) can be regarded as a compromise between monism and pluralism. As we shall see, at the root of the disagreement between these philosophical perspectives were different accounts both of what exists and of what it means for something to exist.

EXISTENCE

'What really exists and what does it mean to say that something exists?' This question still perplexes philosophers today, and it was a central concern of philosophers in classical India. Of the *āstika darśanas*, the Nyāya and the Vaiśeṣika were the most preoccupied by these questions about Being, or **ontology** (an ontology is a theory about what there is). As we saw in the previous chapter, their position can be described as naïve realism, although some would prefer to call it direct realism. They argued for what can be called a common-sense view of reality, attempting to justify our belief that the things in the world exist much as we experience them and independently of our perception of them. We examine the Nyāya-Vaiśeṣika view further below, but first we consider a position – also maintained within the *āstika* camp – that argues for the opposite view on these central issues.

MONISM

This section focuses on the Vedānta tradition ('Vedānta' means 'end of the *Vedas*'; this is sometimes interpreted as 'the goal towards which the *Vedas* lead'). Like the Mīmāṁsā *darśana* with which it is closely aligned, Vedānta is principally concerned with exegesis – in other words, drawing the meaning out – of the *Vedas*. But the two *darśanas* differ in a crucial respect. Whereas Mīmāṁsā supports a pluralistic view of the reality of the world of our experience, Vedāntins argue that monism is the view which is faithful to Vedic teaching.

Vedānta becomes recognizable as a systematic development of some key *Upaniṣadic* themes between 500 and 200 BCE. There are three main early textual sources for Vedānta ideas: the *Upaniṣads*, the *Vedānta Sūtra* and the *Bhagavad-gītā*. The *Vedānta Sūtra* (also known as the *Brahma Sūtra* or the *Sariraka Sūtra*) is the foundational work of this school. The text we have today dates from the first century CE, although its origins are much older. It is conventionally attributed to Bādarāyaṇa. The individual sūtras are extremely compressed and cannot be understood without a commentary.

The *Vedānta Sūtra* has four chapters; the first focuses on the theory of Brahman and explores questions about the ultimate nature of reality. The text is concerned to counter the popular Sāṁkhya view, which we consider below, about the relationship between consciousness and matter. The Sāṁkhya argued for the dualist position that reality is the product of the interaction of two things: consciousness (*puruṣa*) and matter (*prakṛti*). According to the *Vedānta Sūtra*, Brahman alone is the cause of the universe and ātman is part of Brahman.

Different philosophers proceeded to develop the key ideas of the Vedānta *darśana* in various ways. The three most well-known commentators are Śaṇkara (788–820? CE), Rāmānuja (*c.*1017–1137) and Madhva (1197–1276 CE). Discussion here focuses on Śaṇkara, the earliest of these commentators, as his system has proven to be the most influential in the long run. Both Rāmānuja and Madhva developed their views in response to Śaṇkara's interpretation of the Vedic heritage.

When western scholars started taking an interest in the philosophies of India during the nineteenth century, it was Śaṇkara's version of Vedānta that they first encountered. Śaṇkara's monist philosophy seemed to have a natural affinity to monotheism, and thus it appealed to nineteenth-century western Christians. Subsequently there was a tendency to portray Vedānta as the culmination of philosophy in India and this view was widely accepted by Indian thinkers as well as western ones. Nowadays scholars tend to be more aware of the rich variety of philosophies that flourished in India and are more cautious about portraying Vedānta as the final word.

ADVAITA VEDĀNTA

Śaṇkara remains one of the most well-known Indian philosophers. Despite being one of the most creative systematizers in the history of Indian thought, he claimed to be a faithful representative of the Vedic tradition. Many of his ideas can be traced back to the *Māṇḍūkya Upaniṣad* (*Sourcebook*: 55f.). Śaṇkara's philosophical system is known as Advaita Vedānta ('*advaita*' simply means non-dual). His theory is advanced in the form of a detailed commentary on the *Vedānta Sūtra* (*Sourcebook*: 509–21). Much of Śaṇkara's writings were devoted to convincing his readers that his was the correct interpretation of the *Vedas*. Recognizing that much in the ancient textual material did not easily fit into his monist understanding of reality, he proposed that within the sacred texts there are two levels of truth, a conventional or pragmatic level on which we can make claims about the many things in the world of our experience, and a more fundamental level on which we can make claims about the ultimate reality of Brahman. Śaṇkara seems to have taken this two-level theory of truth from earlier Buddhist thinkers and, as we shall see below, this is not the only aspect of his theory that is indebted to them (King 1997: 120–26).

To understand Śaṇkara's position it is helpful to look at two key passages from the *Chāndogya Upaniṣad*, each of which had a shaping role on his thought; again, Uddalāka Āruṇi is instructing his son Śvetaketu:

> 'It is like this, son. By means of just one lump of clay one would perceive everything made of clay – the transformation is a verbal handle, a name – while the reality is just this; "It's clay."'
>
> (6.1.4, in Olivelle 1998: 247)

> 'In the beginning, son, this world was simply what is existent [i.e., Brahman] – one only, without a second. ... And it thought to itself: "Let me become many. Let me propagate myself."'
>
> (6.2.1 and 3, in ibid.)

Śaṇkara is a monist not only because, in accordance with the first of these passages, he claims that the world of our experience has one origin – Brahman – but also because he claims, following the second passage, that Brahman remains the one absolute reality. He interpreted this second passage to mean that everything else that exists is dependent on Brahman and is less real. Nonetheless, employing his two-level theory of truth, he can still affirm that the material world of our experience is 'real', and that we can make true claims about it. It is just not ultimately real, so our claims about it will only possess 'conventional truth'.

In advancing this monist interpretation of the Vedic tradition, Śaṇkara opposes the views of a number of earlier thinkers, both *āstika* and *nāstika*. I have already explained that he rejects the pluralist view held by the Nyāya-Vaiśeṣika and Mīmāṁsā *darśanas*. Although he agrees with the claims they make about the world of our experience, he adds the proviso that if those claims are true, they are true only at the conventional level. I have also mentioned above that he proposes his view as a rival to the dualism of the Sāṁkhya and Yoga *darśanas*. But Śaṇkara has another target besides these; he is keen to reject a number of Buddhist positions that, at first sight, seem remarkably similar to his own. In particular, by claiming that the material world is real although not ultimately real, he rejects the theory that was popular among Buddhists (following Nāgārjuna) that the world neither exists nor does not exist, as well as the view – which was associated with the Buddhist Yogācāra *darśana* – that what we take to be the material world is just a product of our consciousness. Given that his position runs contrary to the views of so many other thinkers, the onus was on Śaṇkara to provide good reasons for his view to be preferred over those of his rivals.

Much of Śaṇkara's argumentation is focused on an attempt to explain the connection between Brahman and the material world. His key move is to distinguish between *Saguṇa Brahman* (Brahman with qualities) and *Nirguṇa Brahman* (qualityless Brahman). Brahman as the absolute reality is qualityless and does not interact with the material world. *Saguṇa Brahman*, however, is represented through human categories of thought as Īśvara – a personal God. Although the material world depends on *Nirguṇa Brahman* for its existence, employing the two-level theory of truth explained above, *Saguṇa Brahman* (as Īśvara) is thought to be the creator and governor of the world. Śaṇkara's system can be represented as follows, with the highest level of reality at the top.

Layer 1: Absolute reality.
Nirguṇa Brahman, Qualityless Brahman, Brahman/Ātman.
Layer 2: Absolute reality seen through categories imposed by human thought.
Saguṇa Brahman, Brahman with qualities. Creator and governor of the world and a personal god (Īśvara).
Layer 3: Conventional reality.
The material world, which includes 'empirical' selves.

Despite apparently having three layers, Śaṇkara's system is monist because all that is not Brahman (the absolutely real) is dependent upon Brahman. But Advaita Vedāntins do not deny that we have sensory experience and that when we perceive something we perceive something that is, in some sense, real. At the conventional level they can claim that we are in fact perceiving what we appear to be perceiving; while at the ultimate level they would say that what we appear to be perceiving is not what is actually there.

Consider this scenario:

1 There is no snake in the corner.
2 Motilal sincerely reports, based on his sensory experience, 'I see a snake in the corner'.
3 What really is in the corner is only a coil of rope.

Such cases in which we misidentify what we are perceiving are quite common and Śaṇkara uses this fact to make his own position seem plausible. But the simple scenario outlined above does not seem to capture what is distinctive about Śaṇkara's position. This is because he is not claiming that in each case of sensory perception we are mistaking one thing for another thing, such as a rope for a snake. Rather he claims that under normal conditions sensory perception does tell us what really exists at a conventional level. It is only if we were to take it as a source of information about the ultimately real that we would be mistaken. On Śaṇkara's view, at the ultimate level the world which we encounter through our senses is not much different from a hallucination and can be compared to the 'world' we experience in dreams. At this deep level, there just is no mind-independent physical world to which our senses could give us access.

After denying the ultimate reality of the mind-independent physical world, Śaṇkara goes even further, adding the radical claim that our minds are not ultimately real either. But the argument does not stop there. If only qualityless Brahman exists and I exist, then I must be qualityless Brahman. We return to Śaṇkara's theory of the self in the following chapter.

In effect, although Śaṇkara's conclusions may seem implausible at first sight, he has arrived at his position by employing a distinction that is familiar to philosophers the world over, namely, the distinction between reality (*nirguṇa Brahman*) and appearance (the world of physical objects, persons and a personal God). What gives this argument its power is that, as we saw above with the example of the rope and the snake, it is easy to come up with examples in which the way something appears to our senses leads us to false conclusions about the way that thing actually is. This is one way to generate philosophical scepticism, and it is by appealing to our experience of such perceptual illusions and combining this with his interpretation of the Vedic teachings about Brahman that Śaṇkara arrives at his distinctive view.

Intriguing though Śaṇkara's theory is, there remain questions about whether or not it is a logically consistent theory. Some modern critics are inclined to dismiss the theory summarily on the grounds that it entails a contradiction and thus could not even possibly be true. Keith Yandell, for example, argues that Advaita Vedānta requires one to hold the following two logically contradictory claims: 'that something exists but altogether lacks properties, and that something that altogether lacks properties can be identical to a variety of things that have properties and are distinct from one another' (Yandell 1999: 242).

Behind this criticism is the view that for an entity to exist it must have at least one property, for to exist just is to have at least one property. One potential way to respond would be to claim that existence itself is a property (contra Immanuel Kant); but a response more in keeping with the core of Śaṇkara's view would be that at the ultimate level there just are no properties as properties only occur at the level of experience. At least then Śaṇkara would not seem to be guilty of another logical mistake that Yandell accuses him of. His claim that 'Brahman is ātman' need not commit him to holding that Brahman has all the properties that ātman has in the realm of conventional reality. So Śaṇkara's ability to distinguish between what one says about ultimate reality and what one says about conventional reality, combined with his two-level theory of truth, allows him to evade the kind of criticism posed by Yandell.

Nonetheless, the claim that Brahman exists without any qualities at all does remain hard to swallow. Part of the difficulty is that once one has asserted it there seems to be nothing else to be said at the level of ultimate truth about Brahman or about the relation between Brahman and the world of conventional reality. This was a criticism developed by the later Vedāntin, Rāmānuja, to whose theory we now briefly turn.

VIŚIṢṬĀDVAITA VEDĀNTA

Rāmānuja's version of Vedānta is known as *Viśiṣṭādvaita Vedānta*. This is usually translated as 'qualified non-dualism' or 'non-dualism of the qualified'. Although it is in the same philosophical tradition as Śaṇkara's theory, and also claims to be a form of monism, Rāmānuja's theory departs from Śaṇkara's on a number of key issues.

Rāmānuja claims that Brahman cannot exist without the existence of human selves and without the material world. He also denies Śaṇkara's claim that Brahman could exist without qualities, instead holding that the qualities of Brahman are real in an absolute sense. On Rāmānuja's view it is important to be able to affirm that, for example, Brahman really does have the quality of compassion and that this is not just a projection of human minds.

According to Rāmānuja, the absolutely real is a trinity of Brahman (as a personal God), a plurality of selves and the material world. These three together form a unity in which selves and the material world are portrayed as Brahman's body. Brahman is the cause of the existence of selves and the material world. However, in creating them Brahman has transformed itself into these things in an absolute sense. Hence, Brahman has become dependent upon them. Each of these items is thought of as ultimately real in the sense that none can be reduced to the others. Nor could any one of them exist without each of the others. This is what Rāmānuja means by the claim that, at the most fundamental level, reality contains a qualified non-duality (in other words, a qualified monism).

Rāmānuja seems to have arrived at this view as a result of his attempt to respond to Śaṇkara's claim that everything we routinely experience, including ourselves, is illusory. We saw above that even the God Īśvara, on Śaṇkara's view, was illusory. Rāmānuja believed that this was an inadequate religious conception and he sought to replace it with a theory that, while remaining within the tradition of Vedic monism, nonetheless could acknowledge the genuine reality of the things presented to us in our experience.

Given their opposing philosophical views, it should come as no surprise that these thinkers defended different accounts of the goal of the religious and philosophical life, although they both called it by the same name: liberation ('*mokṣa*' in Sanskrit). According to Śaṇkara, liberation was achieved when ātman realized that it was already united with qualityless Brahman. In one's ignorance one had thought that one was an individual separate from Brahman and living in a real material world. Liberation comes from the knowledge that this is not the case; based on this knowledge ātman can dissolve back into Brahman. Rāmānuja's picture is rather different. He denies that liberation involves dissolution of the ātman into Brahman, claiming instead that it is a state of freedom from ignorance in which one is aware of one's essential nature and of one's relationship to Brahman.

Clearly, Rāmānuja's so-called 'qualified non-dualism' depends on being on the right side of a fine distinction separating dualism from monism. However, he has been accused of adhering to dualism in practise while only paying lip service to monism. Credibility for his, perhaps, tenuous position no doubt came from the fact remarked upon above that the Vedic tradition itself contains a dualist stream: it is to this which we now turn.

DUALISM

As explained above, the Sāṁkhya and Yoga *darśanas* are united in the conviction that at the most fundamental level only two things exist: namely, *puruṣa* (pure consciousness) and *prakṛti* (primordial matter). We next review the Sāṁkhya's position before turning to that of the Yoga *darśana*.

SĀṀKHYA

The ideas that form the core of the Sāṁkhya *darśana* are among the most ancient found in the Indian traditions, although the earliest extant Sāṁkhya text, the *Sāṁkhya Kārikā* of Īśvarakṛṣṇa, dates from the fourth–fifth century CE. The term 'Sāṁkhya', when used to refer to this *darśana*, means 'enumeration'. The principal interest of philosophers of this school was to enumerate the variety of physical and non-physical phenomena that constitute the world. This interest was not, of course, merely academic, as is made clear in the opening line of the *Sāṁkhya Kārikā*: 'From torment by three-fold misery arises the inquiry into the means of terminating it' (*Sourcebook*: 426). And, as the text goes on to explain, the way to overcome suffering is to learn to discriminate between one's genuine self and what one mistakenly believes to be oneself. The way to accomplish this is thought to lie in careful enumeration of everything that exists so that one can successfully discriminate between which of these things are the real you and which aren't. Again, the *Sāṁkhya Kārikā* states: 'Thus, from analysis of the principles (*tattva*), knowledge arises that "I am not, nor does it belong to me, nor do I [as an empirical or conventional self] exist". This [knowledge] is free from error, pure and abstract' (*Sāṁkhya Kārikā*, sūtra 64; cited in King 1999: 185).

In seeking to enumerate all the constituents of our world, the Sāṁkhya developed a complex theory of the world's evolution which purported to explain how each type of thing is the product of some other type of thing. They claimed, for instance, that our capacities of sense – hearing, feeling, seeing, tasting and smelling – evolved from the ego (the sense we have of being a self), which itself is an evolutionary product, once removed, from primordial matter (see the diagram showing the stages of the evolutionary scheme in King 1999: 175). The Sāṁkhya held that prior to the onset of the evolutionary process only two types of substance existed and these were *puruṣa* (pure consciousness) and *prakṛti* (primordial matter). They took it to follow that everything which later came into existence is ultimately derived from an interaction between these two substances.

According to the Sāṁkhya, *prakṛti* is the actual primordial stuff out of which the world evolves. However, on its own it would not have generated the world because it has no power to do so. *Prakṛti* can be imagined as an inert mass of dark matter that only becomes active when *puruṣa* starts taking an interest in it. When this happens the evolutionary process is triggered and then unfolds through a series of stages. The first stage involves the manifestation within *prakṛti* of three *guṇas* – the categories, or *tattvas* (literally, 'that-ness'), which will become foundational to each aspect of the universe of our experience. The *guṇas* are: qualities of light (*sattva*), of passion or energy (*rajas*) and of darkness or inertia (*tamas*). The subsequent stages of evolution are said to be kept in balance by the three *guṇas*. The theory of *guṇas* became very important to later thinkers both within and without the Sāṁkhya *darśana*. In time each *guṇa* came to be associated with a particular social class as well as a different type of food (that is, 'cool', *sattva*; 'hot', *rajas*; and 'dulling', *tamas*). (On the *guṇas* see Flood 1996: 234f.)

The Sāṁkhya do not give an explanation of why the pure consciousness that is named *puruṣa* suddenly attended to the inert mass of *prakṛti*. They seem to regard this as, what we might call, a cosmic blip that had the dramatic but unintended result of setting in train the evolutionary process which led to the manifestation of the world of our experience. The Sāṁkhya deploy this evolutionary scheme to give an account of the existence and nature of both the world and of each individual consciousness within that world.

Clearly, there is a deep dualism within Sāṁkhya thought. But unlike the forms of dualism that dominated western philosophy, the duality is not that of mind and body. Rather, as we have seen, Sāṁkhya dualism posits two fundamental, non-reducible types of substance – pure consciousness (*puruṣa*) and primordial matter (*prakṛti*). What the Sāṁkhya understand by 'pure consciousness' is not what is generally understood by the English term 'mind'. In fact, as is commonly the case within Indian philosophies, the Sāṁkhya regard mind as a modification of the body. The mind is thought of as a synthetic power whose main function is to organize the information derived from the senses. Mind is not taken to be equivalent to the underlying ego (or sense of being a self) which is thought to be logically prior to embodiment. But just as the Sāṁkhya would never claim that the true self was the mind, they would not claim that the ego was the true self either. The ego is the psychological subject lodged within the material body – the subject we refer to when we use the first person predicate 'I' – however, this is not the true self. The genuine self is described as a silent witness who is fundamentally different from the embodied self. The latter is sometimes referred to as the empirical self because it is the subject – the owner – of 'our' experiences. And, as we have seen, the existence of the empirical, embodied self is explained as the by-product of the process of evolution which primordial matter (*prakṛti*) has undergone. The empirical self is thought to be lodged within the realm of *prakṛti*, while the true self is beyond in the realm of *puruṣa*.

On the basis of their evolutionary schema then, the Sāṁkhya arrived at the belief that the true self of each individual is in reality free and only superficially connected with matter. The *Sāṁkhya Kārikā* states: 'not any spirit is bound or liberated, nor does any migrate; it is Primal Nature, abiding in manifold forms, that is bound, is liberated, and migrates' (*Sāṁkhya Kārikā*, sūtra 62; *Sourcebook*: 444). Realization of one's essential freedom, this *darśana* proclaims, can be facilitated through acquiring the right kind of knowledge. Unsurprisingly, the first step is to understand the teachings of the Sāṁkhya *darśana*. However, the knowledge that brings about the realization of freedom will not be entirely theoretical, but will also be practical. The practical dimension was brought to the fore in the yoga traditions, to which we now turn.

YOGA

As explained earlier, the term 'yoga' is used to refer to a variety of spiritual and philosophical practices. These include both mental disciplines, such as meditation, and physical exercises structured around various postures ('*asanas*' in Sanskrit). We saw above that one meaning of the term 'yoga' is 'to yoke'. What is supposed to be yoked to what differs according to the underlying metaphysical system accepted by various forms of yoga. The goal of yogic practices might be conceived as being to merge ātman and Brahman, or alternatively, in theistically oriented traditions, as uniting ātman with God. However the overall goal is conceived, yoga traditions claim that the means to attain the goal lies in achieving a state of harmony between the physical and non-physical components of one's being. Inner harmony, which includes the cessation of discursive thought, is regarded as a necessary means to final liberation.

Stilling the mind is thought to be of vital importance because the activities of the mind are believed to entrap us in a seriously mistaken view of both the world and the self. The *Yoga Sūtra* states: '*Yoga* is the restraint of mental modifications (chapter 1, verse 2; *Sourcebook*: 454). The mind is at work continuously giving us the impression that we are actors in the world of our experience. However, according to yoga philosophy, which follows the Sāṁkhya on this point, our true self is fundamentally different from the empirical self – the ego that seems to be the psychological subject of experiences. Prior to our learning how to discriminate the true self from the empirical self, our true self is lost in the story of our life. It is as if we have become so totally absorbed in a movie or book that we identify with the characters and lose all sense of our genuine identity. By stilling the mind we can begin to break our identification with the empirical self and learn to recognize our true self – a *puruṣa*. The practice of yoga is supposed to ease us out of the ignorance we have fallen into and thus break our identification with the false idea of the self that had previously taken possession of us.

The Yoga *darśana* accepts the Sāṁkhya's evolutionary schema along with the theory of the *guṇas*. Yoga teachings are concerned with the more pragmatic issues of how to acquire the practical knowledge that will lead to release from the phenomenal world in which the true self appears to be trapped. The aim of the school is to explain and teach the method by means of which the self can be purified and hence liberated. The practitioner is to learn how to understand and control the different elements of the human person, both physical and psychical.

Yoga was a distinctly recognizable *darśana* by the third century CE when the *Yoga Sūtra* was finalized (it is of uncertain authorship but is traditionally ascribed to Patañjali). However, the origins of the school lie much further back in time. As we saw above, the earliest written evidence of the importance of the practice of yoga in the cultural milieu of ancient India is found in the *Upaniṣads*, and it is likely that this practice is even older than those texts.

The *Yoga Sūtra* is less overtly philosophical than the *Sūtras* of the other *darśanas*. This is probably because thinkers in the Yoga *darśana* accepted the basic philosophical presuppositions of the Sāṁkhya. Their text is best described as the fruit of generations of yogic practice rather than as the product of lengthy philosophical debate. It is really a manual for practice for the dedicated yogic practitioner. As such it goes into great detail about a wide variety of mental states the practitioner might encounter. For those who have not experienced these states, and who are not engaged in the attempt to do so, the *Yoga Sūtra* can be a difficult text to engage with.

Despite its historical affinity with Sāṁkhya, as mentioned above, Yoga teachings are compatible with a range of metaphysical beliefs. One notable idea over which Sāṁkhya and yoga differ is that of the existence of God. Sāṁkhya is an atheistic *darśana* while yoga is theistic (see *Yoga Sūtra*, 1.23–28). Yoga regards Īśvara as a special kind of *puruṣa*, one that has never become entangled in matter. This theistic idea became particularly important from the sixteenth century; but that is a story that cannot be told here.

So far in this chapter we have looked at two accounts of the fundamental nature of reality and we have seen that both are elaborations of ideas found in the *Vedas*. The next theory we examine also claims to be a faithful expression of the Vedic understanding of reality, although it differs in startling ways from both of the theories considered above.

PLURALISM

Pluralists about ontology hold that monism and dualism are false because reality is constituted by a plurality of different kinds of items that cannot be reduced to just one or two types of entity or substance. As mentioned above, a number of *āstika darśanas* adopted pluralism: namely, Mīmāṁsā, Nyāya and Vaiśeṣika. Of these the latter had the most developed view and the other schools adopted its way of thinking about ontological questions.

VAIŚEṢIKA

The name of this *darśana* is derived from the Sanskrit term '*visesa*' which means 'particularity'. This tells us that Vaiśeṣika thinkers were interested in the various individual items which make up the world and feature in our experience of it. According to the Vaiśeṣika, nine basic substances can be distinguished, namely: earth, water, fire, air, ether, space, time, self and mind. The first four of these are regarded as basic material substances (see *Vaiśeṣika Sūtra*, books I and II, in *Sourcebook*: 387–91; and King 1999: 106), and the remaining five are thought to be basic immaterial substances. They claimed that careful analysis of our experience shows that everything that there is must be composed of one or more of these nine basic substances – even though we cannot actually experience instantiations of some of these substances directly.

The Vaiśeṣika did not claim, however, that these substances were the most fundamental level of reality. Instead they believed that substances were composite and were constituted by atoms. On their view, nothing is smaller or more fundamental than an atom. Material substances were thought to be constituted by material substance atoms which themselves came in four kinds: earth atoms, water atoms, fire atoms and air atoms. Likewise, immaterial substances were said to be composed of immaterial substance atoms that were thought to exist in five kinds: ether atoms, space atoms, time atoms, self atoms and mind atoms. (Each mind was regarded as one mind atom.) Everything that exists then – at the most fundamental level – was thought to be made up of combinations of atoms; when these combinations disintegrate finite things cease to exist. Each existing object is composed of a collection of atoms which forms one or more of the basic substances of earth, water, fire or air. Differences between objects were held to be the result of different ratios obtaining between the basic substances that compose them. Despite their importance to the theory, the Vaiśeṣika acknowledged that atoms are not perceivable individually, so we have to infer their existence. Moreover, each atom was postulated to be eternal and indestructible (you will recall the Jaina's treatment of the idea of stability discussed in the previous chapter).

Key to the Vaiśeṣika's approach was a scheme of 'categories' within which everything that there is was thought to have a place (this scheme can be compared to a similar one developed in the West by Aristotle). They proposed that everything must be analyzable into one or more of the following seven categories:

- Substance
- Quality or attribute
- Action or motion
- Universality
- Particularity
- The relation of inherence
- Absence.

These seven categories allow us to speak of three different ways in which something might be real (see King 1999: 105–15). Things in the first three categories are said to be 'existent'. The term 'existence', then, only applies to things in the categories of substance, quality or attribute, or action or motion. But this is not to claim that items in the other categories aren't real. The Vaiśeṣika held that everything is real if it falls into at least one of the categories. Items in the next three categories – universality, particularity and the relation of inherence – cannot be said to exist, but they are nevertheless 'real'. The Vaiśeṣika speak of 'real presences', arguing that if something can be known then it must be real in some sense. This last claim led them, sometime after proposing the first six categories, to add the seventh category – absence – to their scheme. In order to explain the knowability of the lack of something, they believed that they had to regard the absence as a reality. To get the idea, think of the experience you would have if your dog went missing. His absence would surely be tangible. Such considerations led the Vaiśeṣika to argue for absence as a genuine category of reality.

The Vaiśeṣika's theory is intricate and complex; but this is unsurprising given that its purpose was to provide a pluralist analysis of the nature of reality that could account for everything falling within our experience. Given this responsiveness to actual experience you might have expected that substances – such as earth and water – would be the most fundamental entities in the Vaiśeṣika ontology. But, as we have seen, this is not the case. In fact, the Vaiśeṣika held that we cannot directly perceive substances at all but only the qualities, such as colour and taste, that inhere in them. It is on the basis of our perception of qualities that we infer that substances exist. What underwrites the inference from the existence of qualities to the existence of substances is the conviction that qualities cannot occur without a substance in which they inhere (for example, a colour is always a colour of something). Buddhist philosophers proved to be especially critical of this conviction, arguing that we are not entitled to regard anything as real if we cannot – even in principle – ever experience it.

Although the Vaiśeṣika had initially proposed the categories as a way of making sense of the world perceived through our senses, as the Buddhist critics pointed out, they had been led to postulate the existence of realities which cannot be directly perceived and hence can only be known by inference – such as atoms and substances. Moreover, it became apparent that atoms and the category of substance were not the only troublesome items in this respect. The Vaiśeṣika categories of universality and the relation of inherence also lacked direct points of contact with our experience. Buddhist philosophers objected to this luxuriant ontology that went far beyond our possible experience and they developed a number of alternative views in their attempts to provide a more parsimonious account of what really exists.

EXPERIENCE

Despite their acute differences the three accounts of the fundamental nature of reality (that is, monism, dualism and pluralism) that we have examined above are each compatible with the character of our actual experience. Those holding these rival accounts are clearly not proposing different descriptions of what our experience of the world is like. Instead they hold different views on the wider theoretical framework within which our experience should be interpreted. This suggests that whatever the correct theory of the nature of reality is, it is not revealed to us directly through our experience of the world. More worryingly, if our actual experience really is compatible with a number of different theories then that experience is unlikely to tell us which of the competing theories, if any, is the correct one.

Of all the *darśanas* considered so far in this chapter, Advaita Vedānta seems to have taken most seriously the lesson that theory must go beyond experience, although this realization is also at work in the other theories we have examined insofar as they all posit things that we cannot, even in principle, ever experience directly, such as inherence and substance. In the following section we briefly explore some Buddhist ways of thinking about the fundamental nature of reality. As we shall see, while Buddhist philosophers were especially reluctant to give up on the data delivered to us through our experience, they too arrived at theories which held that – at the ultimate level – reality is very different from anything that we ever actually experience.

THE NATURE OF THINGS

The period between the third century BCE and the second century CE is sometimes referred to as the scholastic period of Buddhist thought. The tradition of Buddhist scholarship that developed during this period is known as Abhidharma. Philosophers in this tradition entered into the debate about ontology with enthusiasm, developing elegant and complex positions that rivalled those of the *āstika darśanas*. As we will see in the next chapter, the Buddha had taught that everything is characterized by impermanence. An ontology based on permanently existing atoms would seem to be fundamentally incompatible with this teaching. Hence Buddhist philosophers urgently needed to provide an alternative to the Vaiśeṣika's theory.

As we saw above, the Vaiśeṣika had proposed atoms to be the most fundamental level of reality; Abhidharmikas held that place to be occupied by what they called *dharmas* ('*dharma*' is a technical term in Sanskrit used to refer to the most basic element of reality – whatever that may be). While Abhidharmikas agreed that *dharmas* were what are immediately present in experience, their disagreement about the nature of these *dharmas* was so intractable that it led to a schism within Buddhism in the mid-third century BCE. Ironically, the view of the Sarvāstivādins that became dominant within Buddhism after the schism was the very position that earlier had been judged non-Buddhist (King 1997: 91–98). The Sarvāstivādins held that although *dharmas* were momentary within experience, each possessed an eternal unchanging essence (*svabhāva*). Other Buddhists found this position uncomfortably close to that of the Vaiśeṣika and worried that it introduced a contradiction into the heart of Buddhism. The challenge of reconciling Buddhist ontology and the teaching of the historical Buddha was taken up by philosophers belonging to another stream of Buddhism.

MAHĀYĀNA

Between the first century BCE and the first century CE Mahāyāna Buddhism began to distinguish itself from other Buddhist traditions (see Williams 1989). Early Mahāyānins criticized the Sarvāstivādin's *dharma* theory on the grounds that it portrayed *dharmas* as rather too much like very small things that were not subject to change. In other words, according to the Mahāyānins, the Sarvāstivādin's version of Abhidharma had failed to provide a sufficiently robust account of the distinction between *dharmas* and the Vaiśeṣika's atoms.

A rival theory was proposed which took seriously the idea that impermanence is more basic than permanence. The argument was that if, at the most basic level, reality is impermanent, it follows that reality is fundamentally constituted by events and not by permanently existing entities. The smallest unit of reality was hence taken to be a micro-event; and some Mahāyānins claimed that these micro-events were the *dharmas* sought by the various Abhidharmika traditions. According to this theory, our world is not really populated by the things that we seem to experience. Instead, at the most fundamental level, reality consists of *dharmas* or micro-events. In any moment of experience there could be thousands of these occurring.

Mahāyānins argued that the idea that reality is constituted by only momentarily existing *dharmas* is an extension of the basic Buddhist conviction that nothing is permanent (to which we return in the following chapter). Madhyamaka Buddhists, following Nāgārjuna, drew out what they took to be the further implications of this idea and claimed that *dharmas* were 'empty' of being (*svabhāva*) because they lacked independent existence. They took it to follow from this that – despite appearances to the contrary – there can be no change, in any conventional sense of the word 'change'. Momentary *dharmas* cannot be subject to change for change requires real entities persisting for more than a moment. This led them to the somewhat unintuitive conclusion that, although ultimately nothing is permanent, nothing really changes and nothing ever really occurs.

ULTIMATE REALITY

What is the ultimate nature of reality then? We have surveyed here a number of alternative views each of which emphasized a different aspect of our experience of the world. Śaṇkara's monism moved from the observation that our experience is sometimes misleading to the claim that it is always misleading. Sāṁkhya dualism asserts that the origin of everything we experience can be traced back to two irreducibly real things: *puruṣa* and *prakṛti*. Vaiśeṣika pluralism attempts to take the reality of what we are given in experience more seriously and seeks ways to explain and categorize it. But, as we have seen, this led the Vaiśeṣika to posit the existence of things which we cannot experience and to deny the existence of things we ordinarily take ourselves to be experiencing, like tables and chairs. The same problems affected Buddhist attempts to explain what is really present in our experience. Some, such as the Yogācārin Vasubandhu (fourth or fifth century CE), embraced these problems and, biting the bullet, claimed that what is given in experience is nothing but a 'conscious event'. Later Yogācārins were to conclude that the world of our experience is a product of the mind, hence this form of Buddhist philosophy is alternatively known as Cittamātra, which can be translated as Mind Only (see Williams 1989: chapter 4). We meet it again in Chapter 6. Every one of these views might incline us to believe that our actual experience is a dubious foundation upon which to build a theory about the ultimate nature of reality.

The debate about ontology between Buddhist philosophers and those in the *āstika darśanas* went on for over a millennium. It is closely related to the arguments about knowledge considered in the previous chapter. As we shall see in the following chapter, it is also closely related to arguments about the identity of the true self. It has already become apparent, especially in the discussion of Yoga, that each theory about the nature of reality examined in this chapter has implications for how the true self is conceptualized. We examine some of the contending theories in the next chapter.

SUMMARY OF CHAPTER 2

This chapter began with a brief discussion of pre-philosophical speculation about the origin of the world (and of selves) found in the *Ṛg Veda* and the *Upaniṣads*. This led into an examination of the main contending views within classical Indian philosophy on the fundamental nature of reality: monism (the Advaita Vedānta position), dualism (the Sāṁkhya/Yoga position) and pluralism (the Nyāya/Vaiśeṣika position). These views were explained and relevant arguments considered.

We then saw that one challenge faced by each of these views was to give a satisfactory account of our everyday experience of the world. In attempting to take this experience seriously Buddhist philosophers arrived at a view according to which, at the most fundamental level, reality is nothing at all like the way it seems to be. In the following chapter we pick up some of these themes again as we turn to theories about the identity of the true self.

REFERENCES AND FURTHER READING

PRIMARY TEXTS

Patrick Olivelle, *The Early Upaniṣads: Annotated Text and Translation* (New York: OUP, 1998). Selections from the *Upaniṣads* are also in *Sourcebook*, pp. 37–96.

Īśvarakṛṣṇa's *Sāṃkhya Kārikā*. In *Sourcebook*, pp. 426–45.

Kaṇāda's *Vaiśeṣika Sūtra*. In *Sourcebook*, pp. 387–97.

Patañjali's *Yoga Sūtra*. In *Sourcebook*, pp. 454–85.

Rāmānuja, *The Vedānta-Sūtras with the Commentary of Rāmānuja*, trans. George Thibaut, Sacred Books of the East, vol. 48 (Middlesex: The Echo Library, 2006).

Śaṇkara, *The Vedānta-Sūtras*, with the Commentary of Śaṇkarācarya, trans. George Thibaut, Sacred Books of the East, volumes 34 and 38 (New Delhi: Motilal Banarsidass).

R. C. Zaehner (trans. and ed.), *Hindu Scriptures* (London: J. M. Dent & Sons, 1966).

SECONDARY LITERATURE

George Dreyfuss, *Recognizing Reality* (Albany: SUNY Press, 1997).

Gavin Flood, *An Introduction to Hinduism* (Cambridge: CUP, 1996).

Wilhelm Halbfass, *On Being What There Is: Classical Vaiśesika and the History of Indian Ontology* (Albany: SUNY Press, 1992).

Richard King, *Indian Philosophy: An Introduction to Hindu and Buddhist Thought* (Edinburgh: Edinburgh University Press, 1999). See chapter 8 on Sāṁkhya and Yoga.

——, *Early Advaita Vedānta and Buddhism* (Delhi: Sri Satguru Publications, 1997). Not for beginners, but see chapters 3–5 on Madhyamaka and Yogācāra.

G. Larson, *Classical Samkhya* (Delhi: Motilal Banarsidass, 1979).

Bimal Krishna Matilal, *Logic, Language and Reality* (Dehli: Motilal Banarsidass, 1985).

Karl Potter (ed.), *Encyclopedia of Indian Philosophies*, 8 volumes (Delhi: Motilal Banarsidass, 1983–). See volume 2.

Paul Williams, *Mahāyāna Buddhism: The Doctrinal Foundations* (London and New York: Routledge, 1989).

Keith Yandell, *Philosophy of Religion: A Contemporary Introduction* (London and New York: Routledge, 1999).

3

PERSONS

The philosophies that flourished on the Indian subcontinent characteristically drew a firm distinction between the true self and the self that – prior to our liberation from rebirth – we routinely take to be the subject of our lives. Here we consider a sampling of the views supported at one time or another by one *darśana* or another. We begin with the answer given by the Cārvākas to the question 'what is the self?'.

SELF AND WORLD

Theories about the identity and nature of the true self grow organically from other more general philosophical commitments. This is particularly clear in the case of the Cārvākas, as the basic principles of their philosophy – which were examined in Chapter 1 – gave rise to a distinctive understanding of the self and its place within the world.

We have seen that Cārvākas, such as Jayarāśi, advocated systematic philosophical scepticism about all claims that are not directly based on our experience, and they combined this with the belief that the material world that we can experience is the sum total of what really exists. We have also seen that Cārvākas were sceptical about our powers of rational argumentation, and that they were particularly concerned to point out the difficulties facing inferential reasoning.

As most of our purported knowledge is the result of inference, Cārvākas were sceptical about many things which were taken for granted by others. The following passage gives the flavour of the Cārvākas' scepticism and shows the extent to which they were prepared to argue against the generally accepted beliefs of their culture, particularly when those beliefs concerned the self:

> There is no heaven, no final liberation, nor any soul in another world. Nor do the actions of the four castes, orders, etc., produce any real effect. The Agnihotra [fire sacrifice], the three Vedas, the ascetic's three staves, and smearing oneself with ashes, were made by Nature as the livelihood of those destitute of knowledge and manliness. If a beast slain in the Jyotiṣṭoma rite will itself go to heaven, why then does not the sacrificer, forthwith, offer his own father? ... While life remains, let a man live happily, let him feed on ghee [clarified butter] even though he runs in debt; When once the body becomes ashes, how can it ever return again? If he who departs from the body goes to another world, how is it that he comes not back again, restless for love of his kindred? Hence it is only as a means of livelihood that the Brahmans have established here all these ceremonies for the dead – there is no other fruit anywhere. The three authors of the Vedas were buffoons, knaves, and demons.
>
> (In Chattopadhyaya 1994: 254f.; see *Sourcebook*: 233f. The author, Mādhava, is citing the lost *Bṛhaspati Sūtra*)

While this passage rejects some of the most widely accepted views within traditional Indian thought about the self and its future prospects, there is more to it than that. There is a positive philosophy here too. It is what we might call a form of **hedonism**, which counsels enjoyment of the present life. This view can be summed up in the claim that as only this world exists, and there is no survival of death, people should enjoy this life as much as they possibly can.

Most of our knowledge about the Cārvāka *darśana* is derived from works by later thinkers who discuss it critically; principal among these works is the book from which the above quotation is taken – Mādhava's *Sarvadarśanasaṃgraha* (*A Compilation of All Doctrines*). This is a philosophical commentary, compiled in the fourteenth century CE, on the major schools of philosophy in India. In it Mādhava claims that the Cārvākas' philosophy is especially hard to overcome because it tends to be what the unreflective believe anyway. The majority of living beings, so he claims, would join the Cārvākas in declaring:

> While life is yours, live joyously;
> None can escape Death's searching eye:
> When once this frame of ours they burn,
> How shall it ever again return?
> (In Chattopadhyaya 1994: 248;
> see *Sourcebook*: 228)

Cārvākas, then, appeal to supposedly widely held intuitions that this life is all that we have and that this material world is the only reality. To vindicate Mādhava's claim about the pervasiveness of the Cārvākas' basic doctrine we can note that it has striking affinities to **naturalism** and **materialism** – both fashionable theories today.

The Cārvākas, as explained in Chapter 1, were committed to **empiricism** – the view that sense perception is the only legitimate source of knowledge. This led them to hold that all our statements about what exists must be based on sense perception. They then made the further claim which, although it does not strictly follow from the previous one, is a natural extension of it: whatever cannot be perceived does not exist. In other words, they held that only what is accessible to our senses is real. Regarding those things that are accessible to our sense, the Cārvākas believed – along with many in the ancient world, including, as explained in the previous chapter, the Vaiśeṣika – that they were composed of some combination of four elements: earth, water, fire and air.

Applying these ideas to the specific case of the self, the Cārvākas concluded that human beings, like everything else that exists, are composed of a combination of these four elements. As there is nothing else to a person other than what can be perceived, there cannot be an immaterial soul or self forming the core of personhood and which might survive death. Upon death the combination of material elements constituting the person dissolves and that person simply ceases to exist. Just as modern naturalists seek to explain consciousness by reducing it to some set of material constituents, the Cārvākas were aware that they needed to explain how consciousness arose from matter. They attempted to solve this problem by proposing that consciousness is a natural by-product of the combination of the material elements composing the physical body. The emergence of consciousness is explained by comparing it to the way an intoxicating power can emerge from a combination of material components (think, for instance, of the process by which wine or beer is made) none of which possessed that power prior to their combination with the others (see *Sarvadarśanasaṃgraha*, in *Sourcebook*: 230). Extending the analogy, we could say that once the components are again separated the intoxicating power would just disappear. Thus consciousness disappears when the elements making up the physical body are dispersed at death.

Cārvākas attempt to support their theory of the material constitution of the self with the following argument:

> [S]ince in 'I am fat', 'I am lean', these attributes abide in the same subject,
>
> And since fatness, etc., reside only in the body, it alone is the soul and no other. ...
>
> (In Chattopadhyaya 1994: 250; see *Sourcebook*: 230)

This argument seems very modern as it consists of an appeal to the way we use language to talk about ourselves. Cārvākas claim that by employing expressions like 'I am fat' or 'I am lean' we show that we are aware that we just are our body, because such qualities as fatness and leanness are attributes of a physical body. In such expressions the pronoun 'I' must then refer to my body which is, therefore, me.

Cārvākas realized that the phrase 'my body' seems to be a counter-example because it implies that another subject has ownership of the physical body. However, they brush this objection aside with the claim that this use of language is merely metaphorical. Unfortunately, they give no grounds for why we should take examples like 'I am fat' literally and the expression 'my body' metaphorically. There would only be reason to do this if their theory were already established, so this argument is too weak to support the Cārvākas' thesis. Indeed they do not seem to have enjoyed much success in persuading other philosophers to adopt their view, as is evident from the range of contending answers to the question 'What is the self?' that continued to vie with one another for support throughout the classical era of Indian philosophy and into modernity.

SELF IN THE *UPANIṢADS*

This chapter began with a brief account of the Cārvākas' position to make two points. First, that theories about the self emerge from more general theories about the nature of reality; we shall see this illustrated again below when we consider a Buddhist account and the Advaita Vedāntin view. Second, that the philosophies of India contain a number of different and even incompatible theories about the self. There is no single theory that all philosophers would agree with. Nevertheless, with the exception of the Cārvākas, most *darśanas* – *āstika* and *nāstika* alike – share a vocabulary that they use to explain their views. They all talk about 'karma', '*saṃsāra*' and 'liberation', for example. While this shared terminology can disguise the fact that they actually mean very different things by these words, it nonetheless reminds us that each of these perspectives developed from the interpretation of the Vedic tradition pioneered in the *Upaniṣads*.

Many of the *Upaniṣads* are concerned with self-knowledge and promote the belief that attaining it is much more important than merely performing the ritualized acts prescribed by the Vedic tradition. This belief is a hallmark of the transition from Vedic to classical culture and it is present in each of the traditions that derive from the Vedic root – all of which, in the post-*Upaniṣadic* era, held that attaining self-knowledge was the key to liberation: release from the cycle of rebirth.

Alongside the injunction to 'know thyself', the *Upaniṣads* introduced the idea – not found in the earlier Vedic writings – that the self is 'unborn and eternal, primeval and everlasting' and 'is not killed, when the body is killed' (*Kaṭha Upaniṣad* 2.18, in Olivelle 1998: 385; see *Sourcebook*: 45). Essentially, they proposed that the physical body is mortal, while the immaterial self is deathless. The eternal character of the true self is thought to follow from its non-physical nature, which is what enables it to continue to exist without being connected to a material body (*Sourcebook*: 76). In the *Kaṭha Upaniṣad* the self is compared to the driver of a chariot, while the chariot is compared to the physical body: 'Know the self [*ātman*] as a rider in a chariot, and the body, as simply the chariot' (3.3, in Olivelle 1998: 389; see *Sourcebook*: 46). Self and body are separable as are the driver and his chariot. Moreover, just as we expect the driver to be in control of the chariot, we also expect the self to have mastery over the body.

Expanding on this image, the *Kaṭha Upaniṣad* acknowledges that, just as a person might fail to be a good chariot driver by losing control of the vehicle, a person can fail to know his true self and thereby lose control of what happens in his embodied life. To guard against this a tranquil mind and restraint from bad conduct are recommended, as these are prerequisites of self-knowledge:

> Not a man who has not quit his evil ways;
> Nor a man who is not calm or composed;
> Nor even a man who is without a tranquil mind;
> Could ever secure it [i.e. knowledge of ātman] by his mere wit.
> (2.24, in Olivelle 1998: 387; see *Sourcebook*: 46)

As we saw in the previous chapter, various techniques – such as meditation – were developed in ancient India as tools to promote tranquillity of mind and hence self-knowledge (see *Sourcebook*: 49).

The view that the true self is not dependent for its existence on the physical body proved to be very influential, especially when conjoined with the belief that the self is identical to ultimate reality (a belief which we explore further below). Crucially, it drew attention to the possibility that a non-material self could be related to more than one body over a connected sequence of lives.

REBIRTH

Once the self is thought to be eternal and the body transitory, questions inevitably arise about what happens to the self when the body dies. The *Upaniṣads* sought to answer such questions by introducing the idea of rebirth (a notion that is absent from the earlier Vedic literature). The self was thought to transmigrate from body to body, taking on a new one when the old one died. Rebirth was not regarded in a positive light, however. In fact, it is described as 'death after death' (*Sourcebook*: 88). The *Upaniṣads* suggest that once one has found the true self there will be no more rebirth. Clues are offered about how to achieve this:

> On this point there is the following verse:
>
> A man who's attached goes with his action,
> to that very place to which

his mind and character cling.
Reaching the end of his action,
of what ever he has done in this world –
From that world he returns
back to this world,
back to action.

> That is the course of a man who desires. Now, a man who does not desire – who is without desires, who is freed from desires, whose desires are fulfilled, whose only desire is his self – his vital functions (*prāṇa*) do not depart. *Brahman* he is, and to *brahman* he goes.
>
> (*Bṛhadāraṇyaka Upaniṣad* 4.4.6, in Olivelle 1998: 121; see *Sourcebook*: 87)

The key to avoiding rebirth, then, is to free oneself from desire; this will prevent the formation of attachments that would otherwise lead to the performance of actions which ensure another embodied life followed by another death, and so on.

KARMA

The *Upaniṣads* deploy the notion of karma to shed light on the connection between one embodiment and another. To the question 'When a man dies, what is it that does not leave him?', the answer proposed – introduced as a secret not to be spoken of in public – is karma (*Bṛhadāraṇyaka Upaniṣad* 3.3.12, in Olivelle 1998: 81; see *Sourcebook*: 82f.). The belief that karma is the link between one embodiment and another, although not found in the earlier Vedic tradition, came to be almost universally accepted within India. One result of the ubiquity of this belief was that a number of different accounts of karma evolved within the traditions of India. The discussion in this section cannot do justice to all of these accounts. Instead, it deals with them in a general way by employing the terms 'karma-theory' and 'karma-theorist'. These abstractions will allow us to explore a number of the core questions and issues that are relevant to most of the accounts of karma that were on offer in classical India.

Perhaps the most basic idea behind the notion of karma is that all actions have consequences. If we accept that, not unreasonable, claim, we are led to the further idea that moral actions have consequences. From there it is but a short step to saying that good actions have good consequences and bad actions have bad consequences. The intuition behind this last claim is that there is a vital connection between the moral quality of an action (whether it is good or bad) and the consequences of performing it. A person who repeatedly does bad things could expect, according to this view, to experience unpleasant consequences. Conversely, a person who acts well can expect to experience good consequences.

However, it is well known that good things do not always happen to people who have acted well, and in this life, at least, the wicked often seem to be rewarded. These facts are very hard to refute and they seem to provide an argument against the notion of karma outlined above. There is a response though. To explain this unexpected result one simply needs to postulate that the consequences of an action need not be experienced in the same lifetime in which the action is performed. So if we come across a case in which a person who has acted well throughout her life is afflicted by bad things, the karma-theorist can claim that this unfortunate person is now experiencing the consequences of misdeeds performed in an earlier lifetime. The same pattern of explanation can be used to cover cases in which people who perform bad actions enjoy the fruits of their wickedness. The karma-theorist can say that such people will experience the bad consequences of their wickedness, but not until a future life (or, perhaps, later on in the present life).

The karma-theorist maintains, then, that some consequences of actions are experienced in this life and some in future lives. This points us to a key difference between the notion of karma and that of physical causation. Karma is sometimes regarded as a law of moral causation analogous to the law of physical causation. However, the causal law links actions and their effects in a relationship of temporal immediacy. When I drop the vase it shatters immediately, not in a few days or even in a future lifetime. Jayarāśi's objections aside (see Chapter 1), the temporal immediacy of physical causes and their effects usually makes it relatively easy to track the relationship between them. Given some basic scientific knowledge, we can usually come up with a plausible account to explain why a particular cause had the effect that it did. None of this is the case with respect to karma. Because there is often no temporal immediacy between performing a good action and experiencing good consequences, or performing a wicked action and experiencing bad consequences (unless, for example, one is caught by the police while making one's escape with the loot), it is difficult to track the purported connection between karmic cause and karmic effect. Lack of temporal immediacy also makes it very difficult to explain the connection between particular actions and particular effects. Given these difficulties, we might ask what else a karma-theorist might be able to say about the relation between the actions we perform and their consequences.

One view widely held in classical India was that karmic consequences are best understood in terms of *saṃskāras*. These were thought to be the tendencies or, we might say, dispositions which most of us acquire through time and which become embedded within our personality, inclining us to act and think in certain ways. The karma-theorist will claim that these tendencies are the result of actions we have performed in the past. For example, actions motivated by jealousy might cause one to develop a jealous disposition – leading to further actions and thoughts motivated by jealousy and making it progressively harder to choose alternative courses of action. In this way karmic consequences are thought to accumulate in an individual. This idea was already suggested in the claim, found in the *Upaniṣads*, that 'one becomes good by good action, bad by bad action' (*Sourcebook*: 83; see *Bṛhadāraṇyaka Upaniṣad* 3.3.13 and 4.4.5).

This brings to the fore another distinction between physical causation and karmic causation. Namely, that karmic consequences are thought to apply only to the particular individual who performed the act. Things are clearly otherwise in the case of physical causation. If I upset a boulder at the top of a hill it will crush whomever happens to be at the bottom when it comes crashing down into the valley.

That example highlights yet another distinction between karmic and physical causation. When I dislodge the boulder which tumbles down the hill, perhaps killing several climbers and injuring a horse, I may have been trying to rescue my Jack Russell terrier who had become stuck in a rabbit burrow immediately underneath the boulder. My intention had been to do a good deed – rescue my dog. However, the effect was clearly disastrous for those hurt by my action. Karma-theorists would say that although the intentions of an agent are irrelevant to physical consequences, they are relevant to karmic consequences. If I did not intend to kill the climbers and injure the horse, but merely to rescue my dog, then the karmic consequences I eventually experience as a result of my action will have a different character to those which I would have experienced had I actually intended the terrible outcome. (Of course, this easily becomes more complex once we start to consider to what extent I might be morally culpable when, in my eagerness to rescue my dog, I fail to consider the possibility that I might upset the boulder.)

The example of the boulder reveals that the karma-theorist must hold that the same action can have two independent streams of consequences: one physical and one karmic. While all physical actions will have physical consequences, not all of them need have karmic consequences (whether they do or not will depend on the agent's intention). But this distinction raises the problem of explaining the interaction between physical causation and karmic causation. That there must be some interaction is clear because, according to this theory, events in the physical realm affect us in ways that are the result of karma. For example, if my house is washed away by a flood and I lose all my possessions and am reduced to a state of desperate poverty, the karma-theorist will claim that these events in the physical environment had the effect upon me that they did because of my karma. Given that the law of karmic causation is supposed to explain all the experiences (good or bad, pleasurable or painful) that an individual has, an account is needed of the relationship between the physical/environmental realm (in which the water level rose) and the non-material realm of karmic causation. The attempt to provide such an account becomes even more complex when we ask how the theory outlined above can accommodate the idea that our actions are the result of free choices.

> What man turns out to be depends on how he acts and on how he conducts himself. If his actions are good, he will turn into something good. If his actions are bad, he will turn into something bad. And man turns into something good by good action and into something bad by bad action.
>
> (*Bṛhadāraṇyaka Upaniṣad* 4.4.8, in Olivelle 1998: 121; see *Sourcebook*: 87)

Something you can try: Consider your 'present life'. Can you see any causal relationship between your past actions and the way that your personality has developed? Have, for example, generous acts you have performed in the past led you to develop a generous character?

FREEDOM

If what happens to us in the present is the result of what we, or our former selves, did in the past, can we make sense of the idea that we are free to choose how to act now? The karma-theorist might propose that even if everything that happens to us is determined by what we did in the past, we can still have some control about how we will react to the things that do happen. Let's say, for example, that it is karmically inevitable that my house will burn down. When it does happen surely I still have a choice about how to react: I might be angry or I might be resigned, I might even be pleased or relieved that I am no longer a property owner and use the event as an occasion to renounce worldly goods and enter a monastic community. Previously we saw that we can distinguish between two kinds of consequences, physical and karmic. Now it will be helpful to distinguish between the level at which what happens to a person is determined by karma and the level at which that person is free to respond to it in whichever way she chooses. Consider an example provided by Śaṇkara in his commentary on the *Vedānta Sūtra*: a cook requires fuel and water (these are the material conditions of cooking), but once he has them he is free to cook whatever he wants, or even not to cook at all (II.3.37).

It seems that what is being proposed is a theory that is now known as **compatibilism**. As the name suggests, it is the view that freedom and physical **determinism** are not mutually exclusive but are compatible. The idea is that even though all human actions have necessary and sufficient causal conditions, which entails that an agent cannot do other than what he or she does, still free action is possible. What makes an action free is that it is motivated by the person him- or herself. If this were not the case it would be difficult to explain the emphasis in many Indian traditions on practices that are supposed to help us to develop good intentions. Tibetan meditation techniques that are designed to cultivate a compassionate nature in the practitioner are a prominent example.

Despite this, it is undeniable that many texts seem to speak in favour of determinism rather than compatibilism. In the *Bhagavad-gītā*, for example, we find this passage: 'If, in your vanity, you say: "I will not fight", your resolve is in vain. Your own nature will drive you to the act. For you yourself have created the karma that binds you. You are helpless in its power. And you will do that very thing which your ignorance seeks to avoid' (18.59–60, translated by Prabhavananda and Isherwood 2002).

The pronounced emphasis on karmic cause and effect in the traditions of India does not prevent them from claiming that each of us is responsible for our own actions. However, in each successive life we would seem to be even less free than in the previous one, because in each life we become implicated more deeply in the web of karmic causation that binds us. To make matters worse most people have no memories of any past lives. Lacking memories is an impediment to progress because it makes it impossible to learn from what one did wrong in the past and to refrain from doing it again. We seem to be faced with the possibility of repeating the same mistakes over a vast number of successive lives, thus becoming increasingly set in our ways and progressively less likely ever to achieve freedom. In short, as long as we are subject to rebirth we cannot be free – hence the urgency to achieve final liberation.

The point just made about memory raises another puzzle. If the self that undergoes repeated embodiments cannot carry memories across different lives, in what sense is it actually the same individual who is successively reborn? This is especially perplexing if you think, as many people do, that memory is a defining feature of personal identity. So far in this chapter we have skirted around the question of who, or what, is reborn. In the rest of the chapter we examine some rival answers to that question.

INDIVIDUALS

When people in the West think about rebirth they often imagine that it involves an individual person dying and then appearing again in another physical body. But, in view of what has been said above about memory, this simple image is clearly inadequate as an account of how rebirth is understood in the context of Indian traditions.

Consider a case in which we are told that Bill has died and has been reborn as Andrea. Given that Bill and Andrea will each have a different life history, with completely different memories, and will have a sense of themselves as distinct persons, in virtue of what is Andrea said to be a reincarnation of Bill? One answer is that each one of them is the result of the embodiment of the same immaterial self – the ātman. This tells us that, whatever 'ātman' means, it bears very little (if any) relationship to what most of us are accustomed to referring to as our 'self'. In short, the ātman has no memories and no personality. What then is reincarnated?

Below we review a distinctive answer to this question that has been very influential within the philosophies of India, although it is only acceptable to those who are already committed to monism. Pluralists, such as the Vaiśeṣika, and dualists, for instance the Sāṁkhya, offer their own accounts of the self which fit within the context of their respective metaphysical positions. With the possible exception of the Cārvākas', each view of the self proposed by classical Indian philosophers accepts that there is a sharp disjunction between the self of our experience and our true self. As we shall now see, this disjunction is pushed to the extreme by the Advaita Vedāntins.

In the previous chapter we saw that Śaṇkara took seriously the view found in the *Upaniṣads* that ātman and Brahman are, at the most fundamental level, identical. He argued that this must be the case because ultimately only one thing exists. If this view is correct it follows that most people's self-understanding is radically mistaken. Śaṇkara regards such a mistaken self-understanding as a specific instance of the wider delusion which our everyday experience of the world presses upon us. But, as well as being contrary to the common experience of selfhood that many people lay claim to, Śaṇkara's theory also seems to be in tension with the idea of rebirth. If ātman and Brahman are one, what is reborn?

Śaṇkara answers this question by appealing to a distinction between an ātman which is outside the sphere of karmic causation (and thus is totally free) and a 'conventional self' – the *jiva* – which is embedded in the physical world and subject to the laws of karma. But even the *jiva* is not a person as we know persons. It is not identical to any particular individual such as Andrea or Bill. Śaṇkara would claim that what Andrea and Bill have in common is that they are each temporally separated embodiments of the same *jiva*. Andrea was the result of the *jiva*'s association with a material body at a particular time and Bill was the result of a similar association with another material body at an earlier time. According to Śaṇkara, it is the *jiva* that accumulates karma and experiences its effects, not Andrea or Bill. The *jiva* has neither physical nor psychological continuity between its embodiments, nonetheless if we had a full understanding of karmic causation and unlimited knowledge we would be able to identify the karmic continuity between them.

As the *jiva* is part of the world of experience (it is sometimes called the empirical self in English), Śaṇkara will say that it is only conventionally but not ultimately real. The *jiva* then cannot be the true self. In fact, Śaṇkara claims that each *jiva* is the expression of a confused ātman that has lost sight of its genuine nature. The ātman then is the true self and, as such, it is beyond the realm of both karma and experience. Final liberation occurs when the ātman overcomes its confusion and realizes that ultimately there exists no *jivas*, no karma, and no physical world. But when this occurs the ātman apprehends something else. Namely that there is only one ātman and that one's true self is identical to the ultimate, singular and unchanging, reality of Brahman. The illusion of individuality will then finally have been overcome.

According to Śaṇkara really there are no persons, in any sense of the word 'person' that has affinities to common usage. While he does claim that the *jiva* reincarnates, as we have seen, this turns out only to be the case at the conventional level. Despite the fact that Śaṇkara presents his theory as an authentic account of the Vedic teachings, there is a remarkable parallel between his ideas and those propounded by much earlier *nāstika* Buddhist thinkers. In the remainder of this chapter we explore Buddhist thought on the self.

NO ABIDING SELF

Siddhartha Gotama, the founder of Buddhism, lived from 485 to 405 BCE. According to the traditional account of his life, as a young man he was sheltered by his father from suffering and had no exposure to illness, old age or death. When he was finally confronted by these things in his early thirties he was deeply shocked. Seeking an understanding that would allow him to make sense of the suffering he had become aware of, he left his wife and small child and took up a life of strict asceticism. For six years he followed the recommendations of various teachers and then he realized that, despite the many things he had learned, he was no closer to understanding suffering than he had been before.

Finally he sat down under a tree and vowed not to move until he had understood the truth about the human condition. At this point he attained 'enlightenment' and, as a result, became known as the Buddha (which means 'the awakened one'). The tree under which he sat is now known as the Bodhi-tree, the tree of wisdom. Buddhist scriptures contain several accounts of his experience of enlightenment. The following is typical:

> I could see as it really is the primary characteristic of human existence [i.e. suffering], how it arises, that it can cease, and the way leading to its cessation. I knew as they really are the continuity tendencies, their arising, their ceasing, and how to achieve their cessation. Knowing and seeing thus, my mind achieved freedom from the binding effects of holding to opinionated views, and my mind achieved freedom from the binding effects of ignorance. I then knew for certain that I was liberated from rebirth, I had practised what was necessary, done what had to be done, and my present state would generate no further continuity.
>
> (*Vinaya* III.4; Hamilton's paraphrase in 2001: 45)

After his enlightenment the Buddha preached his first sermon and with that began a long career of teaching others what he had learnt about suffering. At the core of his teachings was a view about the true nature of human persons that was radically different from other views in circulation at the time. His view of human persons was embedded within a wider metaphysical theory, central to which were four key insights (known to Buddhists as 'the four noble truths') that – as we can see from the above passage – he had learnt during his enlightenment experience. These insights are: (i) that the primary characteristic of human existence is suffering, (ii) how suffering arises, (iii) that suffering can cease, and (iv) the way leading to its cessation.

The word that is being translated as 'suffering' is '*dukkha*'. Unfortunately, translating this as 'suffering' does not capture its full meaning. As we shall see, '*dukkha*' includes the idea of suffering but encompasses a wider range of meanings than the English word 'suffering' conveys. Some commentators prefer to translate '*dukkha*' as 'unsatisfactoriness' while others simply leave it untranslated.

The Buddha held that the primary characteristic of human existence is *dukkha* because everything within the purview of our possible and actual experience is impermanent. In saying this he was not denying that we were capable of happiness and pleasure. Rather he was drawing attention to the undeniable fact that all of our experiences are transitory. Because of their transitoriness, he claimed, even our most pleasurable experiences have the seed of suffering within them. Consider, for example, the pleasure you might feel upon lying down on a very comfortable bed. The pleasurable sensation might last for a few hours, or even all night. But would it still be there after 24 hours? If you stayed in the bed long enough, your feeling of pleasure would surely turn to discomfort and, if you stayed even longer, you would find yourself in agony.

This simple example concerns physical suffering. But the Buddha believed that the same dynamic was also at work in more complex psychological experiences. Again, for example, suppose that you love somebody very much. You would probably get a great deal of happiness out of your relationship with that person. Now reflect that it is inevitable that the person you love will eventually die. As soon as this happens the *dukkha* within your happiness is revealed. According to the Buddha, all apparently positive emotional states like happiness have *dukkha* within them waiting to emerge when conditions change.

In both of these cases, the physical and the psychological, *dukkha* arises as the result of an inevitable change. But the Buddha also claimed that the causes of suffering ran much deeper than is evident from the kind of examples used above. The underlying problem lies in the attachments we form to transitory states, persons and things. If we are attached to something transitory we will inevitably suffer when it changes or is removed from us. At the root of all this, according to the Buddha, is a false view of the self. Our tendency to form the attachments that bring suffering is generated by a misunderstanding of who, or what, we are as persons. In fact, the most pernicious form of attachment, the Buddha claimed, is our attachment to the belief that we have a permanent unchanging self that is the subject of our attachments. As we shall see, he thought that this view was dangerous because it is one of the principal factors binding us within the cycle of rebirth.

The view that we ourselves are responsible for the arising of *dukkha* is expressed in the second of the Buddha's key insights. Briefly, the origin of *dukkha* is thought to lie in the 'thirst' or 'craving' – we might say, the desire – which leads us to become attached to things like power and possessions. It is desire, then, which gives rise to suffering because, through a causal mechanism hinted at in the third noble truth, desire was thought to lead to rebirth.

The third insight follows closely upon the second: our experience of *dukkha* can cease. The cessation of *dukkha* is known as *nibbana* in Pāli and *nirvāṇa* in Sanskrit; it literally means 'blowing out' and refers to the extinction of the conditions that lead to rebirth. Now if desire is the cause of rebirth, it follows that if one ceases to desire one will have thereby stopped the cycle of rebirth – and this will lead to *nirvāṇa*.

But how does one eliminate desire and thus end the experience of *dukkha*? The answer to this question was the fourth of the Buddha's insights. He taught that what is required is that a person must live according to the Noble Eightfold Path. The elements of this path are:

1 Right Understanding
2 Right Thought
3 Right Speech
4 Right Action
5 Right Livelihood
6 Right Effort
7 Right Mindfulness
8 Right Concentration.

Practically all of the Buddha's teaching was an exposition of this path. He claimed that if each element of the path is pursued, then the person will develop all of the qualities necessary to achieve enlightenment. The ethical elements of the path (those are 3 through to 6) were thought to be no less important than the intellectual ones (1, 2, 7 and 8), and each was to be developed simultaneously not sequentially. Knowledge of Buddhist philosophy which was not accompanied by practice of Buddhist ethical principles was regarded as inadequate to bring about liberation.

We have seen that the Buddha taught that identifying the causes of *dukkha* allows us to prevent those causes from arising and in that way we can solve the problem of suffering. Taking a lead from this basic teaching, early Buddhist philosophy focused on providing a detailed account of the causes underlying our experience of *dukkha.* Because the experience of the self is so intimately connected with the experience of *dukkha,* from its beginnings Buddhist philosophy was concerned to provide an account of what the self is that could replace the false view that was responsible for suffering and rebirth. Following the Buddha's teaching, the core of the Buddhist theory was that no permanent, continuously existing, substantial self underlies our experience (see Gowans 2003: part 2). Instead persons were thought to be aggregates of certain physical and non-physical components that can be categorized as belonging to one of the following five categories (see, for example, *Mahāsatipaṭṭhāna Sutta,* in Walshe 1995: 342):

1 Body.
2 Feelings (specifically, pleasure, pain and indifference).
3 Perceptions.
4 Mental formations/dispositions/tendencies – (these are the bearers of karma).
5 Consciousness – (this is also a bearer of karma).

   Consciousness has three components:

   – abstract mental activity (pure awareness)
   – concrete mental activity (thought about things, ideas)
   – mental functions such as receiving and ordering sense-data, judging, remembering and reasoning.

The Buddhists' claim is that if we carefully analyse our subjective experience of 'ourself' we will be able to identify items belonging to each of the categories in the list above. We will also recognize that all our subjective experience is transitory (see *Sourcebook*: 280f.). Thus, we will realize that none of the items within the range of this experience can be a permanent 'self' (see Rahula 1978: chapter VI). Moreover, further scrutiny of our experience is thought to reveal no other candidates for the 'self' because everything we experience through introspection belongs to one of the five categories.

(Mark Siderits refers to this as the exhaustiveness claim; see Siderits 2007.)

Because of their transitory nature, none of the components given in our experience could be a permanent self, but nor could any collection of them be such a self. The Buddhist position is that there simply is no candidate to be a permanent self: '[I]n the absolute sense there is no ego here to be found' (*Sourcebook*: 284). According to this view, what we commonly call the 'self' is a conventional designation of a supposed collective object (a whole composed of parts). In this respect the 'self' is in the same boat as any other complex object, such as a chariot (see *Sourcebook*: 282–84). What is a chariot except a collection of parts arranged in a certain way? If we analyze the chariot into its parts, we will see that there really is nothing in addition to those parts: the early Buddhists would say that in an absolute sense there is no chariot to be found (as only the parts exist). Despite this we can continue to talk about chariots because to do so is useful. Likewise we can continue to refer to individual persons, like Siddhartha and Bill, because it is convenient for us to do so.

In fact, it is one of the principles of Buddhist philosophy that wholes do not really exist. Table 3.1 gives some examples (*Sourcebook*: 284f). Early Buddhist philosophy claims that, in an absolute sense, only the items on the right side of the table exist. It is our minds that organize these things into wholes, thus apparent collective objects are merely mental constructs.

It soon became apparent, however, that some of the 'parts' – such as those listed in the right side of the table – could themselves be regarded as wholes and broken down into further parts. Just as a city, for example, is composed of houses, a house is composed of

Table 3.1 Some examples of the relationship between wholes and parts

Whole	*Parts*
Chariot	Axle, wheels, pole, etc.
Fist	Fingers and thumb in a certain relation
Lute	Body of the lute, string, etc.
Army	Elephants, horses, etc.
City	Fortification, houses, gates, etc.
Tree	Trunk, branches, leaves, etc., in a certain relation

walls, doors, floors and so on. Early Buddhists seem to have taken this as further evidence that what we regard as a complex whole is responsive to our practical needs. Refining the conception of what a 'part' might be eventually led to the theory of *dharmas* reviewed in the previous chapter.

Buddhists arrived at the conviction that wholes do not exist by way of reflection on the Buddha's insight that everything which exists has a cause of its existence that is outside itself. As nothing is the cause of its own existence, nothing exists independently of that which caused it. In his experience of enlightenment the Buddha claimed to have become aware of the causal relationships, or 'continuity tendencies', that conditioned his own experience and that of others. These continuity tendencies are what determine which particular components will aggregate to form the persons we experience ourselves, respectively, to be.

This led early Buddhists to characterize rebirth as causal continuity between sets of aggregates. From moment to moment the aggregates that form a set are changing. Thus, from one moment to the next there is continuity between what makes up the set, although the set is not completely identical with itself from moment to moment. There is a causal series of continuously changing dispositions and conscious events which constitutes 'personal identity'. We can say that someone is the 'same person' as they were, for instance, five years ago because a series of causally related events connects that person in the present to that person in the past. The basis of personal identity, then, is causal continuity between aggregates. Thus, even in this life we do not have a fixed identity from moment to moment. In a sense, rebirth occurs with each change in the aggregates.

The early Buddhist theory of the self is often interpreted as a denial that the self exists. This interpretation is encouraged by the usual translation of the name of the theory as 'no self' (*anātman* in Sanskrit and *anātta* in Pāli). However, it may be more accurate to translate the Sanskrit and Pāli terms as 'no abiding self'. Indeed, many Buddhist texts make it clear that the Buddha rejected two positions: (1) that the 'self' persists, and (2) that the 'self' is annihilated. Given that he thought both of these positions to be erroneous, it would be odd if he had claimed that upon liberation the self ceases to exist (that would be the 'wicked heresy' of annihilationism; see *Sourcebook*: 286). Here is a passage in which the views rejected are stated and the Buddha's position advanced:

> He, however, who abandons this knowledge of the truth and believes in a living entity must assume either that this living entity will perish or that it will not perish. If he assume that it will not perish, he falls into the heresy of the persistence of existences; or if he assume that it will perish, he falls into that of the annihilation of existences. And why do I say so? Because, just as sour cream has milk as its antecedent, so nothing here exists but what has its own antecedents. To say, 'The living entity persists,' is to fall short of the truth; to say, 'It is annihilated,' is to outrun the truth.
>
> (*Sourcebook*: 285)

Just as we will have no sour cream unless we previously had milk, we will have no self unless we previously had the causal conditions that led to its appearance. The Buddha's claim seems to be that the discussion of whether the self exists or not misses what is really important: namely, understanding the causal pathways that give rise to the experience that we erroneously interpret as belonging to a persisting self.

DEPENDENT CO-ARISING

The key to the Buddhist account of the causal relations that generate our experience of ourselves and of our world is the theory of dependent co-arising (sometimes translated as 'dependent origination', the Pāli is *pratītya samudpāda*). Essentially this is an elaboration of the Buddha's second insight about the arising of *dukkha*, and it is based on the claim that everything that exists has a cause for its existence. The application of this theory to the case of the self is illustrated in the following sequence (see *Sourcebook*: 278; and Rahula 1978: 53ff.):

1 Ignorance generates *karma*. (I.e. the actions one performs in ignorance lead to particular karmic formations, in this sense, *karma* depends upon ignorance for its existence.)
2 *Karma* generates consciousness. (I.e. the karmic formations determine that one will possess consciousness, in this sense, consciousness depends upon *karma* for its existence.)

These first two steps in the sequence apply to the past life and are supposed to explain the mechanism by which a set of causal antecedents gives rise to another embodiment. The next steps (3 to 8) purport to explain the sequence leading to the experience of suffering.

3 Consciousness generates a body. (I.e. body depends upon consciousness for its existence.)
4 Body generates the six organs of sense. (The six organs of sense are: eyes, ears, tongue, nose, skin, mind. These depend upon the body for their existence.)
5 The six organs of sense generate contact. (I.e. without the sense organs there would be no contact with objects in the world. Contact depends upon the sense organs.)
6 Contact generates sensation. (I.e. without contact with objects we would have no sensations. Sensations depend upon contact.)
7 Sensation generates desire. (I.e. we cannot desire objects that we cannot experience. Without sensation there would be no desire, in this sense, desire depends upon sensation for its existence.)
8 Desire generates attachment. (I.e. because we desire things, we become attached to them. If there were no desire, there would be no attachment – desire depends upon attachment for its existence.)

Step 9 takes us into the next embodiment. Steps 10 and 11 give a concise account of the next life that then leads back to the beginning of the sequence, so step 1 is also, in a sense, step 12.

9 Attachment generates continuity. (I.e. our attachment to things generates continuity between one set of aggregates and a future one. If there were no attachment, there would be no continuity.)
10 Continuity generates birth. (I.e. if there were no continuity, there would be no birth. Birth depends on continuity.)
11 Birth generates old age and death, sorrow, lamentation, misery, grief, and despair. (I.e. if there were no birth, there would be no old age, death, and so on. These things depend upon birth for their existence.)

This sequence is found, with minor variations, in a number of early Buddhist texts. It is taken for granted by all Buddhist thinkers, although they do not all interpret it in exactly the same way.

In the previous two chapters we have already been introduced to Nāgārjuna. He is widely regarded as the first philosopher of major importance in the Mahāyāna tradition and, as we have seen, was foundational within the influential Madhyamaka (Middle Way) school of Buddhist philosophy. It was Nāgārjuna who extended Abhidharma theory to incorporate the claim that even the *dharmas* (about which, see the previous chapter) lack an independent existence. In his *Madhyamaka Kārikā* (also known as the *Madhyamaka Śāstra* and the *Mūlamadhyamakārikā, Treatise on the Middle Way*), he stressed the mutual relativity of all things to a far greater degree than had previous Buddhist philosophers. Inspired by an earlier Buddhist text, the *Perfection of Wisdom Sūtras*, Nāgārjuna arrived at his view by providing a new interpretation of the theory of dependent co-arising and drawing out some of the implications which he took to be latent within the earlier statements of the theory.

The *Madhyamaka Kārikā* opens with the claim: 'Nowhere and in no way do entities exist which originate from themselves, from something else, from both, or spontaneously' (*Sourcebook*: 341). The truth of this is implied, Nāgārjuna believes, by the theory of dependent co-arising. And, if it is correct, it follows that all things are 'empty'. Here is his argument:

1 It is not the case that something with 'own being' (*svabhāva*) is produced from itself. (Because what it means to have 'own being' is not to be caused. If any thing had 'own being' it would exist necessarily, causelessly, and hence, eternally.)
2 Nor is it the case that something with 'own being' is produced from something other than itself. (Again, because things with 'own being', if there were any, would not require causes.)
3 Nor could it be produced from both itself and the other. (This follows from the denial of 1 and 2.)
4 Things with 'own being' cannot arise spontaneously. (Because nothing can come from nothing.)

In any case, according to the theory of dependent co-arising, all things are in fact produced by causes. Thus there is nothing causeless, and hence no candidates for possession of 'own being'. Because they require causes, contingent beings cannot be 'own beings'. Thus, dependent co-arising implies that absolutely all things are without 'own being': all *dharmas* are empty (*śūnya*). At bottom, then, the phenomenal world of our experience is 'empty'.

But Nāgārjuna is neither claiming that the objects that furnish our experience exist nor that they do not exist; to say that all things are 'empty' does not mean either of these things. He claims that we go wrong if we think of anything at all (including selves) in terms of existence, non-existence, both existence and non-existence, or neither existence nor non-existence. Adherence to any of these viewpoints implies failure to see the world as it really is.

The correct view of reality recognizes neither entities, selves, nor causes: 'If entities are relative [empty], they have no real existence. The formula "this being, that appears", then loses every meaning' (chapter 1, stanza X, *Sourcebook*: 342). However, in order to make sense of the world of our experience we need to think in terms of entities, selves, and causes. Thinking thus is to think on, what Śaṇkara would have agreed in calling, the conventional level. Likewise, all talk of entities, selves, and causes can only be conventionally true. To think non-conventionally, however, is to recognize that there is no difference between the phenomenal world (that is, *saṃsāra*) and *nirvāṇa*: 'we call this world phenomenal; but just the same is called *nirvāṇa*, when from causality abstracted' (chapter 1, stanza IX, *Sourcebook*: 343; also see stanzas XIX and XX).

LIBERATION

Nāgārjuna's interpretation of the theory of dependent co-arising had led him to claim that '[t]he boundary of *nirvāṇa* is also the boundary of *saṃsāra*, there is not even a subtle difference between them' (*Mūlamadhyama Kakārikā*, chapter 25, stanzas 19–20; in King 1999:124). Insofar as we think of a distinction between them then, it is one put there by the activities of our unenlightened minds (see King 1999: 119–26). Escaping from *saṃsāra* simply requires that we stop regarding it as separate from *nirvāṇa*. This realization would in fact be enlightenment as it would free the enlightened one from further rebirth. We will meet this idea again in Chapter 6.

SUMMARY OF CHAPTER 3

This chapter has introduced some of the main contending theories about the true self proposed within Indian philosophies. After examining the Cārvākas' view, it explained how the concepts of *saṃsāra* (the cycle of rebirth) and karma were commonly understood by philosophers within the post-Vedic traditions. The notion of rebirth formed the context within which all the theories considered in the chapter were developed. After looking at Śaṇkara's account of the identity of the self that is subject to rebirth, discussion turned to the rival Buddhist theory of *anātman* (no abiding self). The arguments in the early Buddhist sources were examined, as well as the interpretations and elaborations of these advanced by the later Buddhist philosopher Nāgārjuna.

This chapter has focused on views of what the true self is. As we turn to the philosophies of China in the following chapters, we will find that questions about human persons are again at the fore, although in China these questions took a less metaphysical and a more practical direction.

REFERENCES AND FURTHER READING

PRIMARY TEXTS

Key readings from the Buddhist traditions are in *Sourcebook*, pp. 272–337. Essential texts of the other schools covered in this chapter are also contained in this anthology.

Mādhava, *Sarvadarśanasaṃgraha*. In *Sourcebook*, pp. 228–34.

Debiprasad Chattopadhyaya (ed.), *Cārvāka/ Lokāyata: An Anthology of Source Materials and Some Recent Studies* (New Delhi: Indian Council of Philosophical Research, 1994).

S. Mayeda, *A Thousand Teachings: The* Upadeśasāhasri *of Śaṇkara* (Albany: SUNY Press, 1992).

Patrick Olivelle, *The Early Upaniṣads: Annotated Text and Translation* (New York: OUP, 1998).

Swami Prabhavananda and Christopher Isherwood (trans.), *Bhagavad-Gita: The Song of God* (New York: Signet Classics, 2002). A readable popular translation.

M. Walshe (trans.), *The Long Discourses of the Buddha: A Translation of the Digha Nikāya* (Somerville, MA: Wisdom Publications, 1995). The *Mahāsatipaṭṭhāna Sutta* is contained in this volume.

SECONDARY LITERATURE

Jay L. Garfield, *The Fundamental Wisdom of the Middle Way* (Albany: SUNY Press, 1986).

Christopher W. Gowans, *Philosophy of the Buddha* (London and New York: Routledge, 2003).

Sue Hamilton, *Indian Philosophy: A Very Short Introduction* (Oxford: OUP, 2001).

Matthew Kapstein, *Reason's Traces* (Somerville, MA: Wisdom Books, 2001).

Richard King, *Indian Philosophy: An Introduction to Hindu and Buddhist Thought* (Edinburgh: Edinburgh University Press, 1999).

E. Lott, *God and the Universe in the Vedāntic Theology of Rāmānuja: A Study in His Use of the Self–Body Analogy* (Chennai: Ramanuja Research Society, 1976).

P. Patil, *Against a Hindu God: Buddhist Philosophy of Religion in India* (New York: Columbia University Press, 2009).

Walpola Rahula, *What the Buddha Taught* (London: Gorden Fraser, 1978).

David Seyfort-Ruegg, *The Literature of the Madhyamaka School of Philosophy in India* (Weidbaden: Otto Harrassowitz, 1981).

Mark Siderits, *Personal Identity and Buddhist Philosophy* (Aldershot: Ashgate, 2004).

——, *Buddhism as Philosophy: An Introduction* (Aldershot: Ashgate, 2007). See chapters 3 and 6.

4

VIRTUE

Attention now shifts from the philosophies of India to those of classical China (*c.*600–200 BCE). The traditions introduced here, and in the next chapter, took shape independently of those covered in the previous three chapters. In Chapter 6 we see cross-fertilization between these two streams of Asian thought, but this was a much later development. Any introduction to Chinese philosophy must mention Kongzi (Confucius), so that is where we begin. Then, after looking at a form of philosophy called Mohism which emerged in opposition to Kongzi's teaching, this chapter introduces two leading early Confucians and examines some of their most important ideas. Key questions addressed in this chapter are: 'Is human nature innately good or bad?' and 'Should an ethical person be impartial?'.

TRADITION

The name 'Confucius' is the Latinized form of 'Kongzi' or 'Kong tzu' ('zi' or 'tzu' is an honorific title meaning 'Sir' or 'Master'). Kongzi (551–479 BCE) lived during the Spring and Autumn Period in the time of the Eastern Zhou dynasty. He is often regarded as the first philosopher of China, despite the fact that he did not present himself as being an original thinker. Seeing his goal as teaching the wisdom, or the Way, of the past to a world that had lost sight of it, he declared: 'I transmit but do not innovate' (*Analects* 7.1, Lau's 2000 translation). In keeping with this statement, he taught his students to value the ways of the past by preserving the traditions that had been handed down from antiquity.

Kongzi believed that the society of his own day had become degenerate and was falling short, both intellectually and culturally, of the standards established in the ideal era of the Western Zhou (*c.*1050–771 BCE). Holding that the reason for this was the loss of ancient wisdom, he devoted his life to rescuing the knowledge of the past from obscurity and to teaching his contemporaries how to live in accordance with the ancient Way. Kongzi emphasized the importance of learning – or scholarship – as the key to understanding the past and preserving traditional values. Hence he regarded himself principally as a teacher and in doing so he set the course for the high value put on education in subsequent Chinese culture. The interest in the past evident in the content of his teaching notwithstanding, it is more accurate to regard Kongzi as a revivalist rather than a traditionalist. He was not concerned simply to reinstate the past and resist change but rather sought to rediscover the deeper meaning of the traditions and values of the past (see Van Norden 2011: 23).

Kongzi initiated an intellectual style which others emulated and, not long after his death, people could refer to the Way of Kongzi and it was clear what they meant. The term 'Confucianism', which has enjoyed wide currency in the West since the seventeenth century, refers to this Way. 'Confucianism' is a translation of 儒家 (*ru jia*), meaning something like the 'school of learning'. While this translation emphasizes Kongzi's interest in scholarship it can give the misleading impression that Confucianism is a movement deliberately started by Kongzi. However, Kongzi never regarded himself as the founder of a movement and it is doubtful that those who aligned themselves with the *ru jia* saw themselves as belonging to one – rather they were in the tradition of the ancient Way, the Way championed by Kongzi.

> If one learns ... but does not think, one will be bewildered. If, on the other hand, one thinks but does not learn ... , one will be imperilled.
>
> (*Analects* 2.15, Lau's 2000 translation)

For Kongzi, learning meant studying texts that were already ancient in his own day. Primary among these was the *Odes* (Book of Poetry). The poems in this collection address a wide range of topics, from love to politics, and Kongzi regarded them as a guide to the ancient Way. However, he did not suggest that memorizing these poems was of primary importance. Instead he believed that they should be creatively deployed to illustrate moral or intellectual problems and used to keep one's independent reflections in a vital relationship to the wisdom of the ancient sages.

The *Odes* is one of the 'Five Confucian Classics' which were the core texts of the Chinese intellectual tradition from Kongzi's time until the twelfth century CE. The other four are the *Book of Changes*, the *Book of History*, the *Book of Rites*, and the *Spring and Autumn Annals*. During the twelfth century, focus shifted away from these Five Classics to the Four Books, namely, the *Greater Learning*, the *Analects*, the *Mencius* and the *Mean*. Instrumental in the shift was Zhu Xi (Chu Hsi, 1130–1200), whose influence within his own culture has been compared to that of Thomas Aquinas in the West. The Four Books became mainstays of education within China until the twentieth century, and generations of young men studied them in hopes of passing the civil service exams. (On Zhu Xi see Gardner 1990 and 2003.)

Very little is known with certainty about the life of Kongzi. It seems that he was born in the state of Lu and, being of noble birth, was well-educated as a youth despite his family's lack of financial means. He became a wandering philosopher travelling from province to province with a group of students. Kongzi seems to have hoped for an official appointment in one of these provinces that would have positioned him to put his philosophy into practice and thereby to bring about social improvements. But he was disappointed and left the one post he briefly occupied in frustration because his advice was not heeded. Some of his students were more fortunate and through their success Kongzi's philosophy came to be a vital shaping force within China and beyond. The influence of this philosophy has persisted into the twenty-first century and even today it is impossible to understand the cultures of East Asia without some knowledge of Kongzi's teaching. This chapter explains the essentials.

As mentioned in the Introduction to this book, there is some dispute about whether Confucianism is a religion or a philosophy. While some forms of later Confucianism do have features usually associated with religions, for example, 'worship' in temples, as far as we know, Kongzi himself did not have much to say about other-worldly 'religious' concerns. His interests were primarily ethical and political. In fact, rather like the historical Buddha, Kongzi seems to have made a firm decision not to discuss certain religious matters. Zilu, one of his students, once asked him to explain his views on ghosts and spirits. Kongzi replied: 'Not yet being able to serve other people, how would you be able to serve the spirits?'. Undeterred, Zilu asked another question: 'May I ask about death?'. Kongzi again replied: 'Not yet understanding life, how could you understand death?' (*Analects* 11.12, Ames and Rosemont's 1999 translation).

This dialogue is from the *Analects* (*Lunyu*), the book on which most of our knowledge of Kongzi's thought is based. It is a collection of short sayings called 'chapters' organized into 20 'books'. Most of the sayings are attributed to Kongzi, although some are attributed to his students. The sayings were collected from notes probably written by Kongzi's students after his death. Current scholarship suggests that the text went through many stages of composition and did not reach its final form until sometime during the Han dynasty (206 BCE to 220 CE). It is generally accepted that chapters 1–9 are the oldest and hence give the most reliable account of Kongzi's teaching.

Perhaps as a result of the length of time over which this work was compiled, many of the sayings are obscure or cryptic when read on their own. Nevertheless, considering the collection as a whole allows us to reconstruct the outlines of a systematic set of ideas. It is apparent that Kongzi was concerned with two connected questions: 'What is the right way to rule?' and 'What is the right way to live?'. A good place to start trying to understand his answers to these questions is with *Analects* 7.6: 'Set your heart upon the Way, rely upon Virtue, lean upon *ren* [Goodness], and explore widely in your cultivation of the arts' (Ivanhoe and Van Norden 2001: 20). This statement can be read as Kongzi's blueprint for an ideal human life. He is saying, 'if you want to have the best kind of life possible, do these things'. Not surprisingly, then, much of the *Analects* concerns the Way, virtue, goodness and the arts.

THE WAY

'*Dao*' (*tao* 道), or 'the Way', was a term widely used during the lifetime of Kongzi and, being associated with different clusters of ideas, it bore a variety of meanings. Perhaps the most basic use of the term was to designate 'the Way' in the sense of a path to follow in order to do something. (Consider how in English it is natural to talk of a way of doing something, like cooking, perhaps.) Generalizing from this basic sense we can arrive at the idea of the Way as a way of living. This seems to have been the sense of the term that preoccupied Kongzi. At a more abstract level still '*dao*' came to mean the fundamental nature of reality, although it does not seem to have had this meaning for Kongzi. As D. C. Lau, a well-respected translator of the *Analects*, puts it: 'The Way … is a highly emotive term and comes very close to the term "Truth" as found in philosophical and religious writings in the West' (Lau 2000: xi).

Although it is impossible to say precisely what Kongzi meant by '*dao*', other than that he saw it as a way of living to be followed by societies as well as by the individuals within them, it is clear that he accorded it a central place in his thought. *Analects* 4.8 is often cited as evidence of this (see text box, 'Translating the *Analects*'). The last two translations of this passage that are given in the text box highlight that the Way is not merely something to be learned, but it is something to be put into practice – it is a Way to be followed. And what it means to follow this Way is intrinsically connected, in Kongzi's view, to the idea of living a virtuous life.

Translating the *Analects*

Understanding what the 'sayings' of Kongzi mean is especially tricky because of the difficulty of translating them into English. Consider, for example, these three translations of *Analects* 4.8:

> Having in the morning learned the Way, one could die that evening without regret.
>
> (Ivanhoe and Van Norden 2001)

> He has not lived in vain who dies in the evening, having been told about the Way in the morning.
>
> (Lau 2000)

> If at dawn you learn of and tread the way, you can face death at dusk.
>
> (Ames and Rosemont 1999)

Which translation should we prefer? Unless we are prepared to put in the time required to learn classical Chinese ourselves, and then, perhaps, come up with our own translations, the best we can do is make use of a number of the available scholarly translations rather than having our interpretation of the *Analects* be dependent on just one. The same applies to all ancient texts.

VIRTUE AND RELATIONSHIPS

'*De*' (*te* 德), or 'virtue', is another concept that Kongzi inherited from the tradition which preceded him. He took over the then commonly accepted idea that virtue is given by heaven, and he taught that it is a person's duty to cultivate it. Only the cultivation of virtue allows a person to lead a good life and to carry out their official role in life well. Following the Way in large part involves cultivating one's virtue. Kongzi believed that rulers and government officials had a particular obligation to cultivate virtue because they could not carry out their tasks adequately unless they were virtuous. He held that possession of virtue was a necessary condition for good leadership, but, more controversially, he also thought that it was a sufficient one. In other words, according to Kongzi, a virtuous ruler will rule the state well simply by being virtuous.

Kongzi believed that it was primarily in the context of family life that people both learned to be virtuous and practised their virtues. Only against the background of a well-ordered domestic life could a person act virtuously in the public domain. Later Confucians attempted to systematize Kongzi's thinking and came up with a list of five principal virtues; these virtues were then correlated to what Kongzi seems to have regarded as the five most important human relationships. The correlation between relationships and virtues can be illustrated as in Table 4.1.

This schema underlines the quintessentially Confucian idea that being embedded in a family is a necessary condition for living a

Table 4.1 Correlation between relationships and virtues

Relationship	*Virtue*
Father/son	Filial piety
Older/younger brother	Brotherly respect
Ruler/subject	Loyalty
Friend/friend	Sincerity
Husband/wife	Submission

good life. To follow the Way requires one to develop and practise whichever virtues are relevant to one's situation and one's family provides the necessary context for doing so. It is noteworthy that, with the exception of the relationship between friends, the relationships listed above are not between social equals. The virtue that is relevant within each of them is practised by the party of lower social standing. For example, the virtue of filiality should be practised by a son in the context of his relationship with his father, if that son has an elder brother then he should cultivate the virtue of brotherly respect towards his elder sibling, as the subject of a ruler the son will also be expected to exhibit the virtue of loyalty with respect to that ruler, and so on.

In addition to the virtues included in the schema, there is another notion – which was introduced above as 'Goodness' – that stands outside of any particular relationships and so can be thought of as more fundamental than any of the individual virtues. We turn to this in the following section.

GOODNESS

The concept '*ren*' (*jen* 仁), which can be translated as goodness, benevolence, humaneness or human-heartedness, was extremely important to Kongzi. This concept takes us beyond any individual virtue because it includes all of them. The person who is *ren* will be virtuous because being *ren* is to have achieved the highest state of human excellence. *Ren* may well be the most distinctive moral concept in the *Analects* and later Confucian tradition. In its broad scope it alerts us to the holistic nature of Kongzi's approach to ethics. Instead of focusing on what individual actions ought to be performed he was concerned with what sort of person one ought to become. This led to a pronounced emphasis on self-cultivation in later Confucianism. But what kind of person must one become to live according to the Way? Kongzi's answer is: one who is *ren*.

Given the role *ren* plays in Kongzi's thinking about the good life, and the fact that it cannot be collapsed into any single virtue, or set of virtues, it is perhaps unsurprising that he does not provide a single explanation of what it means. Rather, there are scattered references to it throughout the *Analects* (the most important passages are 6.7, 6.22, 6.23 and 6.30, 12.1 and 12.2).

There is even some dispute about whether or not Kongzi regarded *ren* as something fully achievable in this life. Some passages suggest that it is possible to be *ren*, whereas other passages portray *ren* as an ideal which it is practically impossible to live up to. In book seven there are two verses which are placed close together in the text despite the fact that they express opposite views on this issue.

> The Master said, 'Is benevolence [*ren*] really far away? No sooner do I desire it than it is here'.
>
> (7.30, Lau's 2000 translation)

> The Master said: 'How dare I claim to be a sage or a benevolent man [*ren*]? Perhaps it might be said of me that I can keep at it without getting tired and go on teaching others without growing weary'.
>
> (7.34, ibid.)

The tension in the *Analects*, then, is between the view that *ren* is within reach if a person can just desire it wholeheartedly and the view that *ren* is a virtually unreachable state of perfection that even the Master himself cannot sustain for long. Despite this tension, we can say that, as Ivanhoe and Van Norden put it: '*ren* designates for Kongzi the quality of the perfectly realized person – one who has so completely mastered the Way that it has become a sort of second nature' (2001: 2). But how is this perfection achieved? Kongzi's answer drew on another core element of his culture.

RITES

The person who is following the Way, and living according to the virtues, leads a life that is structured by the ancient rituals or rites (*li*

禮). In *Analects* 12.1 Kongzi explains how the perfected person, that is, the person who is *ren*, will not do or say anything that is not in accordance with the rites. In fact, in that passage he declares that *ren* just is 'restraining yourself and turning to the rites'. The original meaning of the term *li* was tied to ancient religious rituals in which the rites specified exactly how sacrifices of wine or food were to be made. The scope of *li*, by Kongzi's day, was greatly expanded from this original meaning. The rites covered the minutiae of daily life: from the details of one's dress to the angle of bow appropriate to one's elder brother, and much else besides. Kongzi believed that the practice of the rites had gone into decline and he was keen to re-establish it by emphasizing the role of the rites in living, and striving to live, a perfected life.

Although there was some dispute between later Confucians (particularly followers of Mengzi and Xunzi) about the role of the rites in the moral life, Kongzi's view seems to have been that the rites codified the life of human excellence and by following them exactly one could eventually come to live a perfected life. We might think of the rites as a comprehensive system of moral education; one's education would be complete when one had practised the rites for so long that one now did so without thinking (this is 'spontaneity' in the Confucian sense). In such a case one's own life would have become perfected and one would be *ren*.

Correct practice of the rites was connected, in Kongzi's view, with the correct use of language. This becomes apparent in *Analects* 13.3 when Kongzi is quizzed by one of his students about what his priority would be if he were granted a position of political influence. At first sight, Kongzi's answer is rather surprising: 'It would be, of course, to assure that *ming*, "names", were being applied *zheng*, "correctly"!' When asked to explain his answer, he continues:

> If names are not correct, speech will not be in accordance with actuality; when speech is not in accordance with actuality, things will not be successfully accomplished. When things are not successfully accomplished, ritual practice and music will fail to flourish; when ritual and music fail to flourish, punishments and penalties will miss the mark. And when punishments and penalties miss the mark, the people will be at a loss as to what to do with themselves.
>
> (Ivanhoe and Van Norden 2001: 34f.)

Why does Kongzi make the extraordinary assertion that if language is not used correctly society will fall apart? He seems to think that each thing in the world has a name which expresses its essence. This applies to natural objects as well as relationships. If people lose the ability to use language properly, they will no longer be able to understand the essential nature of things. Kongzi claims that this lack of correlation between the use of words and things themselves will first of all be apparent in ritual and music. Decadence in ritual practice and music are a sign that a society has lost touch with reality; politically and morally the future of such a society would be bleak, in Kongzi's opinion.

Early Confucians followed Kongzi in giving high importance to music. This is an aspect of their world view that many today find difficult to appreciate and it is often passed over with little comment in introductions to Confucianism. However, this is to misrepresent the tradition as excellence in music was regarded as an essential part of self-cultivation. Kongzi was sensitive to the various impacts that different styles of music can have on individuals and social groups. He held that the kind of music enjoyed could be used as a diagnostic tool to judge the moral condition of individuals and societies. But this was not the only function of music in his view; it also had an important didactic and therapeutic role. In *Confucian Reflections*, Philip J. Ivanhoe explores Kongzi's thought about music and draws some insightful comparisons with the ways in which music is used in our own day. (See Ivanhoe forthcoming: chapter 4.)

SELF-CULTIVATION

In Kongzi's view, the people who stood between a society and its potential decay were the *junzi*, 君子, the gentlemen. He held that it is part of the gentleman's function in society to practise the rites and ensure that words are correctly applied to things and thereby to prevent society from degenerating into chaos. The notion of the *junzi* was vitally important to Kongzi. He took a word, '*junzi*', that was in common parlance and gave it a more precise meaning. The word literally meant 'the son of a lord'. When Kongzi adopted this term he dropped the idea that being a gentleman was something hereditary and tied it instead to the way a person behaves. He thought that no one could be a gentleman by birth alone, but that being a gentleman was an ideal to strive for. Essentially it is the gentleman who is on the way to becoming *ren*, and one becomes a gentleman by pursuing *ren*, practising the rites, and becoming a generally cultured and educated person. It is to the person who wants to be a gentleman that Kongzi addresses the advice that we looked at earlier: 'Set your heart upon the Way, rely upon Virtue, lean upon *ren*, and explore widely in your cultivation of the arts' (Ivanhoe and Van Norden 2001: 20).

Much in the *Analects* concerns how to be a gentleman. A gentleman is someone who knows how to behave virtuously and hence knows what is expected of him in all of his relationships. The gentleman is thus a sterling member of any family and a flawless civil servant. And to be both of these things simultaneously is to realize the Confucian ideal.

Notice though that this ideal is completely male-oriented; and here lies what is, perhaps, the most unappealing feature of Confucian philosophy from a modern perspective. A woman could not become a gentleman. In fact, Kongzi had practically nothing to say about women. The most famous passage in the *Analects* to mention women is 17.25:

> The Master said, 'In one's household, it is the women and the small men that are difficult to deal with. If you let them get too close, they become insolent. If you keep them at a distance, they feel badly done by.'
>
> (Lau's 2000 translation)

This suggests that women are an impediment to the gentleman! It seems that Kongzi saw humanity as divided into two groups: one consisting of the gentleman, and the other consisting of the 'small men' (*xiao-ren*), who aren't gentlemen, and women. About those in the second group he had little to say. Many commentators believe that Kongzi's failure to say anything useful about women led to the intensification of a distinctly patriarchal streak in Chinese culture, and later Confucians did little to change this.

As we've seen, Kongzi thought that the proper way to live was to govern one's behaviour by the rites while practising the virtues commensurate with traditional social relationships. It was a powerful message, probably made all the more compelling in the difficult political environment in which he lived and taught. Nonetheless it did not take long before rival philosophical views began to compete with this one for supremacy.

IMPARTIAL CARE

Mozi (Mo-tzu, *c.*480–390 BCE) was the first philosopher we know of to challenge Kongzi's views and argue for an alternative philosophy. Little is known about him personally. However, his familiarity with Kongzi's thought suggests that he was tutored by one of the latter's students, or perhaps a student of a student.

A charismatic leader who gathered an army of idealistic warrior philosophers around him, Mozi had a colourful political career. His army went to the aid of small states which were being threatened by bigger ones. This was consistent with Mozi's political and moral philosophy, which is now often compared to a form of modern, western moral philosophy known as **utilitarianism**. Mozi's principal idea was that impartially pursuing the common good should be every person's aim. He argued that to do this was far more important than taking care of your own or your family's interests.

Some scholars today regard Mozi, not Kongzi, as the key figure behind the emergence of philosophy in China because he introduced a culture of argumentation into the intellectual life of the early classical period (Hansen 1992). Kongzi had no serious rivals and therefore wasn't required to argue for his ideas, but Mozi needed strong arguments for his because he presented them as alternatives to Kongzi's. It is certainly the case that Mozi is the first thinker in China known to us to have realized the importance of a well-structured argument. The school of philosophy he founded is known as the Mohist school (*Mo-jia*) and it was important in its day despite its failure to survive long into the Common Era (it disappeared when Confucianism was adopted as the state ideology during the Han dynasty). Even after the school's demise, Mohist ideas remained in circulation, enjoying a significant impact on those streams of thought which did outlast the turbulent era of the Han.

As we've seen, Kongzi regarded human relationships as determining which virtues ought to be practised in any given situation.

He thought that it was perfectly acceptable, indeed morally required, to treat family members differently than people who were not one's kin and to give preferential treatment to one's friends. Mozi rejected these ideas completely, arguing instead that all people are essentially equal and therefore all should be treated in the same way irrespective of whether or not they are friends or kin. Mozi argued that *jian-ai* (兼爱) was the primary moral concept. This can be translated into English in a number of ways: universal benevolence, universal love or impartial caring, for example. Mozi employed the concept of *jian-ai* to argue against Kongzi's view that one has a moral obligation to put the interests of one's own family and friends above those of other people.

Mozi thought that Kongzi and his later followers were uncritically defending tradition rather than genuinely inquiring about the best way to live. He was the first to realize that questions about what ought to be done are logically distinct from questions about what tradition prescribes. Having made this separation, Mozi sought independent standards of right and wrong conduct and this is what led him to advocate *jian-ai* (see *Mozi*, chapter 16).

Mozi's ideas have come down to us in a book simply known as the *Mozi*. This book exists in various forms, suggesting that subsequent groups of Mohists developed Mozi's ideas in different ways and changed the text to match their interpretation of these ideas; a practice which can be justified on Mohist principles. Mohists believed that tradition had no value just because it was tradition and that any value it did possess was in virtue of its correspondence to correct ideas. So they freely altered the text of the *Mozi*, believing that it would only have value if it contained ideas that could be confirmed independently. If certain of Mozi's original ideas turned out to be false, in the view of the later Mohists, then so much the worse for these ideas.

Mozi himself did not reject all traditional ideas. He held that some of them could be accepted if they passed certain tests. In fact, he proposed a standard of assessment which all claims must meet if they are to be accepted. Mozi explains:

> When one advances claims, one must first establish a standard of assessment. To make claims in the absence of such a standard is like trying to establish on the surface of a spinning potter's wheel where the

> sun will rise and set. Without a fixed standard, one cannot clearly ascertain what is right and wrong or what is beneficial and harmful. And so, in assessing claims, one must use three gauges.
>
> (*Mozi*, chapter 35, in Ivanhoe and Van Norden 2005)

The 'three gauges' are: precedent, evidence and application (a literal English translation of the word rendered here as 'gauge' would be 'gnomon' – an astronomical tool – for an explanation see Van Norden 2011: 63). In examining the precedents of a claim one looks back to the sage kings to see if there is anything in their words or behaviour that supports that claim. This is the aspect of Mozi's thought in which tradition has a legitimate place. However, simply having a precedent in tradition will not be enough to make a claim worthy of acceptance; in his view, it will also have to be assessed by the other two gauges.

The second gauge is evidence. Mozi understood evidence to be 'what the people have heard or seen'. In other words, he suggested that we examine whether or not the claim is supported by people's experience. Does it fit in with a common-sense view of the world? If not, it should probably be rejected. This gauge led him to reject traditional views about fate on the grounds that no one had ever seen or heard fate so there was no reason to believe in its existence.

The final test of a claim is application. This is perhaps the most far-reaching of the three gauges. Mozi proposed that a claim's utility can be assessed by asking: If it is accepted and put into practice, would it benefit the state, families and individuals? He clearly regarded this last test as the most important one, as we will soon see.

Mozi argued that a person can organize his or her life according to one of two basic ideas. First, a person can think that it is absurd to care for people who are not his friends and to whom he is not related. This person will act only to benefit his friends and family. Second, a person can think that he ought to care for all people equally, regardless of whether they are friends or kin. Clearly a person who adopts the first view will live in a very different way from someone who accepts the second view. Mozi thought that Kongzi mistakenly advocated the first view while the second view was the correct one. But Mozi didn't just state his opinion; he provided an interesting argument to defend his point of view. He proposed that we should test each of these claims with the 'three gauges' of precedent, evidence and application.

Relying on the third gauge – application – to establish his position, Mozi recommended that we examine the world and ask ourselves what causes all the trouble we see. Here are some of the harms that Mozi thought required explanation:

> Great states attacking small ones, great families overthrowing small ones, the strong oppressing the weak, the many harrying the few, the cunning deceiving the stupid, the eminent lording it over the humble. ... [In addition, there] are rulers who are not generous, ministers who are not loyal, fathers who are without kindness, and sons who are unfilial, as well as those mean men who, with weapons and knives, poison, fire, and water, seek to injure and undo each other.
>
> (*Mozi*, chapter 16, Watson's translation, in de Bary and Bloom 1999)

He believed that examination would reveal that the cause of these problems lies in people pursuing their own interests and those of their family and friends while neglecting the interests of others. Partiality, then, fails the test of application because when it is put into practice it gives rise to such bad consequences. 'Therefore', concludes Mozi, 'we know that partiality is wrong' (ibid.)

Mozi has argued that it is due to people following Kongzi's principle of partiality, and treating people differently according to their relationship to them, that the world contains so much evil. Now, if the principle of partiality fails the test of 'application', what about the opposite principle – impartial caring or universal benevolence? Mozi speculated that if this latter principle were put into practice the world would be a much better place and everybody would be better off. He writes:

> If men were to regard the states of others as they regard their own, then who would raise up his state to attack the state of another? It would be like attacking his own. If men were to regard the cities of others as they regard their own, then who would raise up his city to attack the city of another? It would be like attacking his own. If men were to regard the families of others as they regard their own, then who would raise up his family to overthrow that of another? It would be like overthrowing his own. Now when states and cities do not attack and make war on each

> other and families and individuals do not overthrow or injure one another – is this a harm or a benefit to the world? Surely it is a benefit.
> (Ibid.)

So the principle of impartial caring would pass the test of application and therefore it is clearly the right principle to adopt.

Mozi has provided a clear and well-structured argument; however, it is vulnerable to an objection that he fails to acknowledge. He puts two claims before us, demonstrates the consequences of adopting each one, and concludes that we should accept the one that has the best consequences. It is as if you were offered a choice of coffee or tea and told that tea would have the consequence of making you feel well whereas coffee would make you overexcited. Would you have to accept the tea? Well, no. You might ask for hot chocolate or water instead, or even say that you are not thirsty. The point is that Mozi's argument becomes less compelling once we realize that he has offered us only two extreme positions, complete partiality or complete impartiality, but there are other options to consider that fall between these extremes.

Nonetheless, given his image of the ideal world in which everyone is impartial, the next question Mozi had to answer was: how to persuade people to put this vision into practice? He believed that intelligent people would be persuaded by the argument we've just looked at. But he also recognized that some people were not capable of organizing their lives according to the conclusion of a good argument. To convince such people he appealed to certain of the religious beliefs common in his day. In particular, he claimed that there is a supreme god (*Shang-di*) who cares for humans and wants them to care for each other, and will punish them if they do not. Mozi believed that this religious sanction would motivate people to practice universal benevolence (see *Mozi*, chapter 31).

Notice what is going on here. Mozi believes that if people hold these religious views, they will put his principle of impartial caring into practice. So he has provided a utilitarian, or pragmatic, justification for accepting religious ideas. Belief in gods and spirits serves a very useful social function and for that reason it ought to be encouraged. (Arguably the gauge of precedent might also lead to the conclusion that gods and spirits exist – the Mohist view on these matters is still a matter of contention today.)

But Mozi can't have been convinced that his argument plus the religious sanction was enough to motivate people to be impartial altruists, for he also argued that a powerful ruler, the Son of Heaven, was necessary to bring it about that everyone lived according to the standards of impartial caring. By means of the enticement of rewards and the threat of punishments the ruler would ensure that everyone behaved impartially and that moral free-riders – those who only act for their own benefit or that of their friends or family – would not go undetected and hence unpunished. Mozi argued that this is the proper function of a ruler and in order to carry it out the ruler would need absolute power (see *Mozi*, chapter 11).

In effect, Mozi popularized the view that people need extrinsic motivations (either rewards or punishments) to act well. Behind this view is the belief that humans do not have a fixed nature that determines how they will act. Mozi firmly believed that behaviour could be moulded in quite dramatic ways simply as a result of someone with enough power and influence decreeing that people should act in a certain way (consider for instance the unnatural practice of foot-binding which was widespread in China into the twentieth century). He concluded that even if impartiality is not natural to humans, our behaviour can be moulded so that we come 'naturally' to impartially care for one another. As we shall see below, this claim sparked a very important debate about human nature that arose when later philosophers sought to defend the Way of Kongzi against criticism.

HUMAN NATURE

Mengzi (*c.*371–289 BCE), who is sometimes known in the West as Mencius, is widely regarded as the second great Confucian thinker after Kongzi (despite the oddity of regarding Kongzi as a 'Confucian' at all!). Mengzi was born about 100 years after Kongzi's death and was a contemporary of the Daoist thinker Zhuangzi (see Chapter 5). Like Kongzi, Mengzi was a wandering teacher who travelled with a group of students. Another similarity between them is that in each case the book connected with their name was originally compiled by their students. What we know about Mengzi comes from the book eponymously entitled the *Mengzi*.

The *Mengzi* is more recognizably philosophical than the *Analects* because, unlike Kongzi, Mengzi had to engage in philosophical arguments with his rivals. By his time different conceptions of the Way had been articulated and defended and were now thriving in a culture of increasingly sophisticated philosophical argumentation. Consequently Mengzi had to clarify and defend his views against alternative theories, and this required that his thought be more systematic than Kongzi's had been. Mengzi aimed to defend the Way of Kongzi against other philosophies that were developing at the time. He regarded Mozi (along with Yang Zhu, whom we consider in the next chapter) as the most serious rival of Kongzi, so he was eager to enter into debate with Mohists (see *Mengzi* 3B9 and 7A26). It is significant that while Mengzi disagreed with the Mohists, his response to them betrays a debt to Mozi's pioneering use of argument.

Mengzi built on the intellectual foundations laid by Kongzi. In doing so he drew out what he took to be some of the unstated implications of Kongzi's ideas. One of these implications, he believed, was that human nature is innately, or inherently, good. Mengzi was led to defend this claim in his attempt to rebut Mozi's view that humans need to be manipulated into acting well by the prospect of reward and the threat of punishment. Against this Mengzi argued that the virtues were natural expressions of our innately good nature.

This claim might, at first sight, not seem remarkably contentious. However, as Mengzi and his fellow Confucians soon discovered, it has far-reaching implications for other things that we believe about the moral life. Part of what Mengzi meant by the claim that human nature is innately good is that human instincts always naturally tend towards good behaviour. He illustrated his claim using what philosophers today would call a thought experiment: asking his students to imagine how people would react to seeing a child about to fall into a well. He thought that everyone's first pre-reflective instinct would be to help the child (see *Mengzi* 2A6), and he took this to show that humans have good instincts, and hence to be evidence supporting his claim that human nature is good. Notice that what is crucial is the spontaneous instinct to help, whether or not this instinct is acted upon is irrelevant to Mengzi's example.

Mengzi has attempted to support his claim about human nature with an argument based on widely available experience (and in this he reveals a further debt to Mozi). Nevertheless, he had to address the obvious problem that plenty of empirical evidence can be mustered to support the opposite claim that human nature is innately bad. Mengzi needed to explain the fact that we often hear about, or even see, people behaving badly. To do so he argued that wicked behaviour is unnatural. In other words, people who behave badly are not acting according to their nature – which is good – but have become corrupted and are acting unnaturally. Mengzi invites us to imagine that the goodness in a person's nature is rather like a collection of sprouts. Given appropriate conditions these moral sprouts will develop, but lacking appropriate conditions they will not (for a further illustration consider the story of Ox Mountain in *Mengzi* 6A8). Expanding on this horticultural metaphor, Mengzi claimed that allowing the innate goodness of our nature to develop is what constitutes self-cultivation.

In *Mengzi* 2A6, after introducing the case of the child and the well, Mengzi proposed that 'humans all have hearts that are not unfeeling towards others'. This is to say that, by nature, we are empathetic towards one another and this inclines us to be altruistic. We are not egoists, solely concerned with our own self-interest, as Mengzi's opponent Yang Zhu seems to have believed (see Chapter 5). On Mengzi's view, the spontaneous inclination to aid the child is motivated by nothing other than an altruistic desire to help. Mengzi drew far-reaching conclusions from this:

> If one is without the heart of compassion, one is not a human. If one is without the heart of disdain, one is not a human. If one is without the heart of deference, one is not a human. If one is without the heart of approval and disapproval, one is not a human.
>
> (2A6, in Ivanhoe and Van Norden 2005)

Scholars argue about how this passage should be interpreted, but many take it at face value to be a definition of what it is to be human. Mengzi claims that humans have four morally relevant dispositions ('hearts' in the above translation), without which they would not be human. These are:

1 compassion;
2 disdain for anyone who does not show compassion;

3 deference to others depending on your relationship to them; and
4 approval of what is good and disapproval of what is bad.

While Mengzi's view that anyone who does not have these four dispositions is not genuinely human may sound implausible, it would be very difficult to disprove. For any apparent case of a human lacking one or more of these dispositions, Mengzi could claim that the person had them potentially if not actually. Given his belief that the dispositions are rooted in human nature, he could also explain cases of their apparent absence by appealing to the idea that something must have interfered with the natural development of the persons concerned.

In fact, Mengzi held that the four dispositions are the tender sprouts of virtue which require nurturing through moral education. The disposition to feel compassion, if correctly nurtured, is the sprout that will grow into the virtue of benevolence. Likewise the disposition to feel disdain in response to failures of compassion is the sprout that, with proper guidance, will grow into the virtue of righteousness. The disposition to show deference to others is the sprout of the virtue of propriety (this is the virtue that consists in correctly performing the rites). Finally, the disposition to approve of what is good and disapprove of what is bad is regarded as the sprout of the virtue of wisdom.

Mengzi has claimed that every human has all four dispositions, or sprouts, but that not everyone develops them. This allowed him to hold that everyone is potentially benevolent, righteous, proprietous and wise, despite the fact that many of us do not actually exhibit all – or, in some cases, any – of these virtues. So, according to Mengzi, although all humans are good by nature, they do not all behave in ways which express this. All sorts of things can go wrong with one's sprouts of goodness and prevent them from developing into virtues. This explains his remark that, '[a]s for what they genuinely are, humans can become good. That is what I mean by calling their natures good. As for their becoming not good, this is not the fault of their potential' (*Mengzi* 6A6).

It is each person's task, then, to nurture the four sprouts of virtue. If a person begins to do this, as Mengzi writes:

> [I]t will be like a fire starting up, a spring coming through. When these are fully developed, he can take under his protection the whole realm

> within the Four Seas, but if he fails to develop them, he will not be able even to serve his parents.
>
> (2A6, Lau's 1970 translation)

Much of Mengzi's teaching was directed to helping his students to develop their sprouts of goodness into actual virtues, and he returns to this theme in many parts of the *Mengzi* (such as 6A7 and 6A8). Significantly, he did not claim that one could learn to be virtuous merely by obeying certain ethical rules, but instead suggested that possession of real virtue requires moral cultivation to the point that one intuitively knows how to behave in any situation.

As explained earlier, by developing his theory of human nature and account of moral behaviour, Mengzi responded to Mozi's criticism of Kongzi. Mozi had advocated impartial caring as an alternative moral approach, and Mengzi aimed to show that Kongzi's was the superior view. He attempted to do this by arguing that Mozi's approach was both impracticable and contrary to human nature because moral education takes place within the context of a family – so it is only natural for people to care more for their kin than for strangers. Against Mozi, Mengzi emphasized Kongzi's claim that whichever virtues it is appropriate to express in a given situation depends upon the status of the people involved and on your relationship to them. Mengzi added the further idea that it is in accordance with human nature to act in this way (see *Mengzi* 7A45).

In advancing these views Mengzi gave a pivotal role to self-knowledge, for if the sprouts of virtue are within one's nature, nurturing them will surely require introspection (that is, focusing on what lies within oneself rather than on the external world). This led him to another idea that is not found in the *Analects*. In fact it led him towards what some commentators have described as mysticism. Here is a key passage: 'Mengzi said, "To fully apply one's heart is to understand one's nature. If one understands one's nature, then one understands Heaven"' (*Mengzi* 7A1; see also 2A2). He seems to be claiming that through introspection one can come to understand one's nature and that this is equivalent to understanding heaven. Mengzi did not think of heaven as the realm of gods or other supernatural entities; rather he regarded it as what we might call the cosmic order. He can be interpreted as claiming, then, that self-knowledge acquired through introspection is the means to achieving harmony with the cosmic order.

Later Confucian thinkers did not pick up on this aspect of Mengzi's thought until many centuries later in the movement known as neo-Confucianism (see Chapter 6). One might regard it as a seed that Mengzi planted in Confucian soil which did not germinate until the intellectual environment was conducive to its growth some 1,000 years after his death. Some of his other ideas had a more immediate effect though. In particular, his theory that human nature was good sparked a lively debate and attracted the criticism of the slightly later Confucian, Xunzi (Hsün-tzu, *c.*340–245 BCE).

Xunzi was the last great Confucian teacher of the classical period. Like Mengzi, he defended the Way of Kongzi against rival views – such as Mohism – that were popular during his lifetime. But, unlike Mengzi, he was also concerned to preserve his own tradition from error. His writings make it quite clear that he regarded Mengzi's views on human nature and moral education as deeply mistaken. We saw that, in responding to Mozi, Mengzi argued that human nature is innately good. This gave the impression (although Mengzi doesn't seem to have intended it) that moral education, including training in the rites, was not strictly necessary to becoming a virtuous person, because the virtues would sprout naturally if not interfered with. Xunzi regarded this as a dangerous misunderstanding of Kongzi's view and he sought to correct it.

The disagreement between Mengzi and Xunzi has often been portrayed as a dispute about whether or not human nature is innately good. In opposition to Mengzi, Xunzi declared: 'People's nature is bad. Their goodness is a matter of deliberate effort' (Hutton's translation in Ivanhoe and Van Norden 2005: 298). However, it seems that the disagreement between them runs even deeper than this: they each advanced different understandings of the purpose of moral education and the means of self-cultivation (see Ivanhoe 2000: chapters 2 and 3).

Xunzi argued that without deliberate effort (*wei*) a human being would not develop the virtues. In his view, rigorous moral training (in large part constituted by practising the rites), as well as scholarship, is required if a person is to get beyond their natural endowment and become virtuous (see Xunzi's essay 'Human Nature is Bad' in Ivanhoe and Van Norden 2005). Stated this way his view does not seem inconsistent with Mengzi's belief that dispositions to moral behaviour are like sprouts that require careful nurturing to flourish. In fact, both philosophers agree about the need for appropriate moral education, although they differ in where the emphasis falls in their thought. Xunzi focused on how bad a person will be if he does not receive moral formation and Mengzi focused on how good a person will be if he does.

As we have seen, Mengzi held that human nature is innately good and he took it to follow that moral education simply requires allowing that nature to develop while removing any impediments to natural growth. In contrast, Xunzi believed that by nature we are all inclined to be egoists and we can only suppress our innate selfishness through a concerted effort to achieve self-mastery. This belief led to the emphasis on rigorous moral education and deliberate self-cultivation found in his writings.

Because of his disagreement with Mengzi, for a long time Xunzi was regarded with suspicion by others in the Confucian tradition, consequently his ideas never became as central to that tradition as did those of Mengzi. Nonetheless Xunzi was the principal spokesman of Confucianism during his lifetime, and, as noted above, he was keen to defend Confucianism against its opponents. Like Mengzi he was critical of Mohism, and he also strove to establish the superiority of Confucianism over other rival views. In the final section of this chapter we explore further the views of Kongzi, Mozi, Mengzi and Xunzi by considering the extent to which their positions promoted **altruism**.

ALTRUISM

Altruists are those who act with the intention of helping others. The similarities and differences between the views of the philosophers introduced in this chapter can be examined by briefly considering their respective stances towards altruism.

Kongzi held that how one ought to behave was governed by certain well-defined social rules. Which of these rules applied at any given time was determined by which individuals would be affected by a proposed action. On this view, the key facts relevant to an individual's decision about how to act were facts about that individual's relationship to other people – principally family members and friends.

For example, if I were faced with two people who needed my assistance equally urgently and one of them was my father while the other was not my kin, then Kongzi would advise me that I ought to help my father *because* he was my father. While this position does not exclude altruism, it does not place it at the top of the moral agenda.

We have seen that Mozi argued forcibly against Kongzi's view, claiming that our moral obligations extend well outside the circle of our friends and kin and that we have a duty to care for others in the same way that we care for our relatives and friends. The best way to take care of one's kin, Mozi proposed, is impartially to pursue the benefit of everyone. He offered several arguments in support of his position, the most striking being that the consequences of adopting Kongzi's view would be harmful to society as a whole. It is to the benefit of everyone, he claimed, for each individual to act impartially towards all others rather than promoting the interests of his own family and friends over those of others. Mozi is clearly making a strong case for altruism.

Mozi's position was an appealing one, and it drew popular support during his lifetime. In defending Kongzi's approach against Mohism, Mengzi sought to demonstrate that Mozi had oversimplified Kongzi's view and that, when properly understood, it was not as narrowly focused on friends and family as Mozi had portrayed it as being. As we have seen, Mengzi's strategy was to emphasize the innate potential for goodness within all humans. According to him, we will naturally act in a way that furthers the good for others – irrespective of whether or not they are our friends or kin. The thought experiment of the child about to fall into the well is meant to establish that altruism is an expression of human nature.

Xunzi was less confident than Mengzi about how readily a person would act altruistically unless that person had already enjoyed a robust moral education that would have shaped his or her behaviour in appropriate ways. Without such an education Xunzi thought that most humans would not go beyond egoism – holding that the right thing to do is what serves their own interests. He believed that only with the right upbringing would individuals be inclined to act altruistically, although even then their moral priorities would still be centred on their kin. Both Mengzi and Xunzi, in contrast to Mozi, thought that this was quite natural because we first learn how to behave well in the context of our family life. 'Morality' and 'family' are consequently inseparable concepts for both of these Confucian thinkers.

The dispute between Confucians and Mohists was premised on different views of human nature which were aligned with divergent accounts of the Way to live, in other words, of the Dao. In the next chapter we see how Daoist thinkers entered this debate with their own views of human nature and conceptions of the Dao. A key point of contention between these schools of thought (and others which we have not considered here) was the way in which human nature could be fully expressed. Confucians advocated a Way of moral education through scholarship and practising the rites, because they thought that the perfected self could only emerge as a result of careful cultivation. Mohists advocated behavioural manipulation through threats and rewards. And, as we shall soon see, Daoists argued that the authentic self could only emerge through avoiding artificial social constraints: the Xunzian notion of deliberate effort was thus anathema to them.

SUMMARY OF CHAPTER 4

We began with a discussion of the importance Kongzi accorded to tradition. The next sections explained key ideas found in the *Analects*: goodness (*ren*), the rites and the relevance of specific human relationships to the virtuous life. Early Confucian philosophy was especially concerned with self-cultivation. However, Confucians were criticized for being too focused on individuals and their immediate friends and family. Mohists argued against Kongzi that a genuinely ethical person would act impartially, not favouring their own interests or those of their friends and family over the interests of others. In other words, they argued that the ethical person should practise impartial caring. The arguments between these two rival schools of thought have been considered, with particular attention to Mengzi's defence of the Way of Kongzi in response to Mozi's criticisms. The section on human nature examined Mengzi's arguments and explained how his position attracted the criticism of the later Confucian, Xunzi. Mengzi and Xunzi disagreed about whether human nature was innately good or not. The final section summarized the divergent views brought to the table so far by considering where each of the philosophers reviewed stood with respect to altruism.

The material in this chapter on Confucian understandings of self-cultivation and human nature prepares the ground for Chapter 5, which focuses on Daoist conceptions of these matters, conceptions which were explicitly developed in critical dialogue with Confucian thought.

REFERENCES AND FURTHER READING

PRIMARY TEXTS

Key sections of the main texts discussed in this chapter (*Analects*, *Mozi*, *Mengzi*, and the writings of Xunzi) are in Philip J. Ivanhoe and Bryan W. Van Norden, *Readings in Classical Chinese Philosophy*, 2nd edition (Indianapolis: Hackett, 2005). Some of the quotations are from the 1st edition: Philip J. Ivanhoe and Bryan W. Van Norden, *Readings in Classical Chinese Philosophy* (New York: Seven Bridges Press, 2001).

Another good translation of the *Analects* is by D. C. Lau (Hong Kong: The Chinese University Press, 2000). See also his translation of the *Mencius* (Harmondsworth: Penguin, 1970).

Also of interest is *The Analects of Confucius: A Philosophical Translation*, translated by Roger T. Ames and Henry Rosemont, Jr (New York: Random House, 1999).

Bryan W. Van Norden (ed.), *Mengzi: With Selections from Traditional Commentaries* (Indianapolis: Hackett, 2008).

For the full text of the *Mozi*, see Ian Johnston's *The Mozi: A Complete Translation* (New York: Columbia University Press, 2010).

The *Odes, History*, and *Spring and Autumn Annals* are translated in James Legge, *The Chinese Classics*, 5 volumes (Taibei: SMC Publishing, 1991).

Another useful anthology is Wm. Theodore de Bary and Irene Bloom (eds), *Sources of Chinese Traditions: From Earliest Times to 1600* (New York: Columbia University Press, 1999). The extracts used in the chapter from Burton Watson's translation of *The Mozi* are to be found here.

SECONDARY LITERATURE

Daniel K. Gardner, *Chu Hsi: Learning to Be a Sage* (Berkeley and Los Angeles: University of California Press, 1990).

——, *Zhu Xi's Reading of the Analects* (New York: University of Columbia Press, 2003).

David A. Hall and Roger T. Ames, *Thinking through Confucius* (Albany: SUNY Press, 1987).

Chad Hansen, *A Daoist History of Chinese Thought: A Philosophical Interpretation* (Oxford: OUP, 1992).

Philip J. Ivanhoe, *Confucian Moral Self Cultivation*, 2nd edition (Indianapolis: Hackett, 2000).

——, *Ethics in the Confucian Tradition: The Thought of Mengzi and Wang Yangming*, 2nd edition (Indianapolis: Hackett, 2002).

——, *Confucian Reflections: Ancient Wisdom for Our Modern Age* (Indianapolis: Hackett, forthcoming).

T. C. Kline and Philip J. Ivanhoe (eds), *Virtue, Nature, and Moral Agency in the* Xunzi (Indianapolis: Hackett, 2000).

JeeLoo Liu, *An Introduction to Chinese Philosophy* (Oxford: Blackwell, 2006), chapters 2–5.

Xiusheng Liu and Philip J. Ivanhoe (eds), *Essays on the Moral Philosophy of Mengzi* (Indianapolis: Hackett, 2002).

Bryan W. Van Norden, *Introduction to Classical Chinese Philosophy* (forthcoming), chapters 2, 3, 4, 6 and 10.

David Wong, 'Mohism: The Founder, Mozi', in Antonio Cua (ed.), *Encyclopedia of Chinese Philosophy* (New York and London: Routledge, 2003), pp. 453–61.

5

AUTHENTICITY

We have seen that in classical China disputes about the right way to live were intimately connected with theories about human nature. Although the views of Confucians and Mohists on such matters were both popular, a number of thinkers disagreed with each camp. After the Warring States Period some of these thinkers were retrospectively termed 'Daoists' because of the especial importance they accorded the notion of the Way in their thought. Prior to this they were not regarded as forming a distinct group (in the way that Confucians and Mohists were). The fact that early Daoists were not part of a movement explains the otherwise puzzling fact that 'Daoist' thinkers do not share a single philosophical perspective and so sometimes advance quite different views. This can be seen by focusing on the variety of answers they gave to two questions: 'How to live an authentic life?' and 'What is the best way to preserve life and avoid injury?'. By looking at some of their answers to these questions this chapter introduces the main concepts of Daoist philosophy while showing how it evolved as a critical response to competing views of the Way, most notably the Way of Kongzi.

What we now know as Daoism emerged in three distinct stages. Most scholars accept that there were certain people contemporary with Kongzi who practised what later came to be identified as Daoism. While they were concerned with problems similar to the ones Kongzi addressed – questions concerning, for example, the best way to live – they differed dramatically in their answers. Most of what is known today about the ideas of these proto-Daoists is learnt from references to them in the *Analects* and the *Mengzi*. In *Analects* 14.41 and 18.5–7, for example, they tease Kongzi for engaging in what they regard as a losing battle: trying to improve both the world and oneself at the same time. Proto-Daoists rejected Kongzi's view that the good life was one shaped by traditional social norms and governed by the rites. Instead they argued that the highest good for a person lay in simply taking care of his own interests and thereby preserving his own life.

EGOISM

Ethical **egoism** is the view that the right thing to do is to pursue one's own interests and thereby maximize one's own good. Within proto-Daoist thought this conviction was combined with psychological egoism – the view that we are naturally inclined to prioritize our own interests. That this combination of views was regarded as a serious rival to Kongzi's teachings is revealed in Mengzi's concern over the popularity of the egoist philosophy of Yang Zhu (Yang Chu, *c.*440–360 BCE), which is evident in his complaint that '[t]he words of Yang Zhu and Mozi fill the world' (*Mengzi* 3B9).

None of Yang Zhu's writings have been preserved. However, from scattered references to him in other texts we learn that he valued life above everything else and that he refused do anything that would endanger his life, no matter how honourable or valuable it would be to do it. Moreover, he argued for this position on the grounds that it accords with human nature, which he took to be characterized by self-interest. He opined that if we are all egoists by nature, then Confucians and Mohists are both wrong because following their ethical recommendations would require a distortion of our selfish nature.

The view that altruism is fundamentally contrary to human nature was popular in classical China and it is in direct opposition to Mengzi's theory (see the previous chapter). Just how popular it must have been is indicated by the fact that the well-respected Confucian, Xunzi, accepted it. Like Yang Zhu, Xunzi argued that humans are naturally self-concerned. However, these two thinkers disagreed on what should be inferred from this. As we have seen, Xunzi advocated moral education, scholarship and rigorous practice of the rites, as the means to overcome this bad nature. Yang Zhu proposed a radically different strategy.

One text from the second century BCE puts Yang Zhu's principal idea like this: 'Preserving life and maintaining what is genuine in it, not allowing things to entangle one's person: this is what Yang Zhu established' (in Fung 1976: 61). The goal, then, is to preserve one's life; but mere preservation is not enough – one must maintain what is genuine in life by avoiding the artificial social and moral constraints recommended by the Confucians and Mohists. The way to do this, according to Yang Zhu, is to not allow things to entangle one's person.

Yang Zhu held that both the Confucians and the Mohists were mistaken in their belief that a well-lived life was one that took place in the midst of social relationships and in service to the state. Instead he claimed that to live authentically requires retreating from society and shunning excessive material possessions and the power that can come from involvement in politics. In short, Yang Zhu proposed that the best life is that of a hermit. Such a life is in harmony with the Dao. This rejection of society found in proto-Daoism had as its converse a valourization of the natural environment. An authentic life was one lived away from towns, in forests or mountains or by the side of a river. The natural world was thought to be the most conducive environment for the authentic expression of human nature. (On the theme of nature within Daoism, see Miller 2005: chapter 8.) This led to a trend found in all subsequent forms of Daoism that, much later, was one of the features making it so appealing first to European Romantics and later to environmentalists.

The idea that preserving life was of principal value was another theme that was to have a lasting place in Daoist thought (in later religious Daoism it emerges as a quest for an elixir of immortality, see ibid., pp. 65–71). As such, it is one of the main legacies of the first stage in the evolution of Daoism – the stage represented by figures such as Yang Zhu. The idea reappears in the two subsequent stages in the development of 'philosophical Daoism' that occurred during the classical era. The major thinkers of each stage attempted to come up with an answer to the quintessentially Daoist question: What is the best way to preserve life and avoid injury? We've seen that Yang Zhu's answer was to escape the world and lead the life of a recluse. Later Daoists did not find this entirely satisfactory and instead they advocated a way of living in the world that combined involvement with detachment.

DAO

Daoists are so named because, despite the fact that in classical China there were many competing conceptions of the Way, they made the Dao the linchpin of their world view. This is especially evident in the second stage of Daoism's evolution, which is represented in what is today the most frequently translated and well-known book from classical China – the *Daodejing* (*Tao Te Ching*). It is to this that we must look to explore the alternative conception of the Dao advanced by the successors of Yang Zhu.

The title *Daodejing* means 'The Classic of Dao and De'; as we have seen, 'dao' can be translated as the Way, and 'de' can be translated as virtue. However, the book is about much more than this title suggests. In fact it engages with the same wide-ranging set of themes that preoccupied other philosophers at that time, and advances distinctive views on human nature and statecraft. Despite these shared topics of interest, the figures associated with Daoism were determined to take a step back from the culture of argumentation that had developed in China. Against Confucians their advice is to '[c]ut off sageliness' and 'abandon wisdom' (chapter 19), and in response to Mohists they assert that '[t]he good do not engage in disputation' (chapter 81). This reaction against argument and learning points to an interpretation of them as focused on what we today might call 'knowing how' (practical knowledge) rather than 'knowing that' (theoretical knowledge). The practical knowledge that they sought was knowledge about how to live in accordance with the Dao, which explains why so much in the *Daodejing* concerns the practical dimensions of life as well as pointed critique of those who are living badly (see chapter 53).

The *Daodejing* was formerly known as the *Lao Tzu*, reflecting the now largely discredited belief that Laozi (Lao Tzu) was its author. It is now clear that the text reached its final form sometime in the second century BCE, although some of the material contained in it is much older, probably dating from the time of Kongzi. In fact, Laozi was traditionally regarded as a contemporary of Kongzi and the founding figure of Daoism; his name literally means 'Old Master'. Nowadays, however, most western scholars accept that he is a mythical construction not a historical figure. The name Laozi is still used for convenience though, as shorthand for 'whoever is responsible for the ideas expressed in the *Daodejing*' and to refer to the representative thinker of the second stage in the development of Daoism.

Chapter 1 of the *Daodejing* is one of the most famous pieces of literature from classical China:

> A way can be a guide, but not a fixed path;
> names can be given, but not permanent labels.
> Nonbeing is called the beginning of heaven and earth;
> being is called the mother of all things.
> Always passionless, thereby observe the subtle;
> ever intent, thereby observe the apparent.
> These two come from the same source but differ in name;
> both are considered mysteries.
> The mystery of mysteries
> is the gateway of marvels.
>
> (Cleary's 2003 translation)

What are we to make of this? The most obvious thing to note is that it is written in verse. In fact, about two-thirds of the *Daodejing* is written in rhyming verse. Why might a philosopher decide to write in verse rather than in the clear prose which, as we know, was already an established form for presenting philosophical ideas at this time? The author, or authors, might have believed that what they wanted to say could not be adequately expressed in language that was supposed to be literally true. What sort of thing is it typically very difficult to express adequately in language? Certain kinds of experience, such as falling in love, might be typically very difficult to put into words.

Perhaps, then, the first chapter of the *Daodejing* is actually a poetic expression of an experience that cannot be described in literal language. The author may have hoped to intimate something of its flavour through poetry. The experience in question is what we might call a mystical experience and it has something to do with the Dao. The poem does not give precise information about the experience, but invites those who hear it to ponder its meaning with a view to facilitating a similar experience in them.

The opening chapter of the *Daodejing* can be interpreted as suggesting that such an extraordinary experience is possible and that it is an experience of the Dao. The Dao, however, remains beyond the grasp of our normal uses of language. Chapter 32 also suggests this interpretation:

> The Way is forever nameless.
> Unhewn wood is insignificant, yet no one in the world can master it.
> ...
> When unhewn wood is carved up, then there are names.
> (Ivanhoe's translation in *Readings*, Ivanhoe and Van Norden 2001)

In itself the Dao is nameless because – although it is the source of everything that exists – it lacks particular qualities. In a favourite Daoist metaphor: the Dao is an unhewn block; all the things that exist are produced from this block when it is carved up. The block itself, or the Dao, cannot be named, but at the same time it is the source from which all nameable things come to be (see also chapter 25). The metaphor of the unhewn block also suggests a different idea. The Dao isn't merely the source of all things (in the way that God in the Christian tradition is regarded as the source of all things); rather the Dao itself takes form in all things. It is as though the Dao were a sort of unformed substance out of which all the individual things that exist are made. Another way of putting this is to say that the Dao is immanent within all things rather than transcendent to them. As we shall now see, this idea had important implications for the Daoist understanding of the natural world.

In the *Daodejing* we are never given a definition of 'Dao'. Instead it is depicted by means of a wide range of metaphors. In chapter 14 we are told that it is '[l]ooked for but not seen' ... 'Listened for but not heard' ... 'Grabbed for but not gotten'. Look in the following chapters for other glimpses of the Dao: 1, 5, 6, 21, 25, 34, 52 and 56.

Notice that in chapter 25 the notion that the Dao is an overarching cosmic principle comes to the fore. This idea is the main connection between the philosophical Daoism examined in this chapter and the forms of religious Daoism that emerged later.

NATURE

I explained above how proto-Daoists, such as Yang Zhu, valued nature as the place where one could live an authentic life away from the dangers of civilization. Later Daoists connected that idea with the further claim that the Dao is immanent in all things, and concluded that by living in harmony with nature a person could experience the Dao. But they took this idea much further than Yang Zhu, in part because by then they had developed a more sophisticated account of nature – according to which 'nature' was in fact everything (heaven, earth, humans, animals, plants and so on). So the ideal of living in harmony with nature required that one live in harmony with the whole of the cosmos. However, to do this one does not necessarily need to live in the woods, because the cosmos is everywhere. The good life then is one that is in harmony with the cosmos and is thereby also in harmony with the Dao. A key part of such harmony is located within the individual – harmony, or balance, is sought both in the body and in the emotions (this idea later fed into traditions of martial arts as well as into traditional Chinese medicine).

PASSIVITY

Harmony, or balance, is not achieved through strenuous activity but requires a certain kind of passivity that will allow one to go along with the flow. The full expression of human nature is then viewed as the result not of deliberate action but of simply allowing it to blossom naturally. The contrast with the Confucian and Mohist views could not be sharper. Daoists regard deliberate effort as inevitably doomed to failure precisely because it is artificial. Thus they criticize Confucians as advising people to seek to express their nature through means which deliberately removed them from what was natural in their nature! The deliberate effort that a Confucian such as Xunzi invested in book learning and the rites would thus be counter-productive on this Daoist view. The *Daodejing* claims: 'When wisdom and intelligence come forth, there is great hypocrisy' (chapter 18).

For the Daoist of the *Daodejing*, integrity, or authenticity, is achieved when one acts spontaneously in accordance with the Dao. As we shall see later, what this means, in practice, is made clear when this view is applied to the realm of human moral behaviour and contrasted with the Confucian perspective (at least 'the Confucian perspective' as portrayed through the lens of the *Daodejing*).

OPPOSITES

The emphasis on harmony and balance in Daoism is linked to an interest in the relation between opposites. A prevalent theme in the *Daodejing* is that opposites tend to produce each other. This theme is evident in chapter 2 (where a number of other core Daoist ideas are introduced):

> Being and non-being produce each other;
> Difficult and easy complete each other;
> Long and short contrast each other;
> High and low distinguish each other;
> Sound and voice harmonize with each other;
> Front and back follow each other.
> Therefore the Sage manages affairs without action (*wu-wei*)
> And spreads doctrines without words.
>
> (Chan 1973: 140)

Perhaps the most famous pair of opposites within later Daoist thought are 'Yin' and 'Yang'. These are represented in the *taiji* symbol now recognized across the globe (Figure 5.1).

The terms 'Yin' and 'Yang' originally referred to the shady side and the sunny side of a hill, but each of them attracted a cluster of other connotations. For example, Yin is associated with passivity, femininity, yielding, darkness, wetness and negativity; and Yang, with action, masculinity, resistance, light, dryness and positivity. Interestingly, at the extreme, Yin qualities are thought to give way to Yang qualities and vice versa. Just as when the sun reaches its maximum extension on one side of the hill we know that that side will soon give way to shade while the other side will brighten, so Yin and Yang are symbols of mutually opposed but nonetheless complementary and correlative forces. The relationship of these forces is such that transformation is inevitable – as one gives way to its opposite – but, crucially, this relationship is also understandable

Figure 5.1 The *taiji* symbol

because the transformation of things follows regular and predictable patterns.

> The idea that too much of something has the opposite to the desired effect may have originated in agricultural experience: too much water (or sun) kills the plant, but so does not enough. Just the right amount is required.

Daoist sensibilities will warn us, then, that where we find an instance of whatever is denoted by one term of a pair of opposites we will also inevitably find an example of what is denoted by the other term, if not immediately then in the future. This applies within nature (winter gives way to spring), to individuals (beauty gives way to ugliness) and states (a good administration inevitably becomes corrupt). It also applies to more abstract concepts such as 'right' and 'wrong', 'virtue' and 'vice'. In the following section we consider how this works.

VICE

In the *Daodejing* the claim that opposites tend to produce each other is deployed to launch a sharp critique of the Way of Kongzi. Confucians are accused of bringing vice into the world as an inevitable result of their attempt to make people virtuous. We consider this claim in more detail now as we turn our attention away from the concept of Dao and towards that of *de* (virtue).

First we need to consider the root meaning of *de* in the context of the *Daodejing*. It isn't quite adequate to translate *de* as virtue because it means much more than the English word 'virtue' does. We saw above that Dao is regarded as the unnameable source of all things which is also immanent in everything. In line with that, *de* can be regarded as the manifestation of Dao in individual things. We can think of *de* as the power of the Dao that is revealed in phenomena. When a thing acts according to its nature, which is the *de* or power of the Dao within it, we can say that it is virtuous. Here, then, being virtuous is equivalent to being genuine or true to one's nature.

Now imagine a human community that lacked the concepts of virtue and vice. The behaviour of the members of this community would simply be natural, no one would categorize it as good or bad. But what would happen if one day someone started using the concept 'virtue'? All of a sudden some actions would be characterized as virtuous and others would not be. But what about the ones that weren't? The way would now be open to characterize them as vices. Now people will strive to be virtuous because there is a recognized standard of virtue to live up to. But inevitably some people will fail to meet this standard, so vice will have come into the world. The point is that the introduction of the concept of virtue brings in its wake the concept of vice. Daoists claim that the community would have been far better off without the concept of virtue. The reason is that the use of this concept – and the striving for virtue that it makes possible – has brought vice into the previously natural and harmonious community.

Several of the poems in the *Daodejing* suggest that virtue (in the Confucian sense) only comes into being as a result of unnatural behaviour. These examples are given in chapter 18:

> When the great Tao declined,
> The doctrines of humanity (*ren*) and righteousness (*i*) arose.

> When knowledge and wisdom appeared,
> There emerged great hypocrisy.
> When the six family relationships are not in harmony,
> There will be the advocacy of filial piety and deep love to children.
> When a country is in disorder,
> There will be praise of loyal ministers.
>
> (Chan 1973: 148f.)

Clearly this poem is meant as a critique of a society dominated by Confucian values and it suggests that the way to overcome social problems is to return to natural behaviour that is unpolluted by ideas of virtue and vice. The Daoist claim is that only when the Way is abandoned do the Confucian virtues of benevolence and righteousness appear. If people lived according to the Way, these artificial virtues would be unnecessary as people would spontaneously follow their natural impulses and those would be in harmony with the natural order. The same analysis is applied to the Confucian virtue of filiality. According to the Daoist view, this virtue is only required when something has upset the natural balance within a family. Again, this analysis is applied to the state. From a Daoist perspective, the loyal ministers that Confucians value so highly are actually a symptom that all is not well in the state.

As we shall now see, the view that virtue and vice generate each other provides a perspective from which to explain the quintessentially Daoist concept of non-action (*wu-wei*).

NON-ACTION

Given the conception of the way the world works found in the *Daodejing*, along with the assessment that the Confucian response to this is inappropriate, the Daoist needs to give some positive account of how to live in accordance with the Dao. We have already considered Yang Zhu's answer to this question and noted that it was not deemed to be adequate by the thinkers represented in the *Daodejing*.

Nonetheless, the answer found in the *Daodejing* elaborates on the idea that harmony with nature is desirable. The *Daodejing* counsels passivity as the way to live in accordance with the Dao, but it acknowledges that passivity alone will not be enough. Something else is required, namely, receptiveness or responsiveness to one's situation. This can be seen in a description of the legendary Daoist Masters found in chapter 15 (see also chapter 22):

> Poised, like one who must ford a stream in winter.
> Cautious, like one who fears his neighbors on every side.
> Reserved, like a visitor.
> Opening up, like ice about to break.
> Honest, like unhewn wood.
> Broad, like a valley.
> Turbid, like muddy water.
> Who can, through stillness, gradually make muddied water clear?
> Who can, through movement, gradually stir to life what has long been still?
> Those who preserve this Way do not desire fullness.
> And, because they are not full, they have no need for renewal.
> (Ivanhoe's translation, *Readings* 2005)

The ideal Daoist aims to bring about certain results and this clearly requires more than passivity and restraint from all action. The aim is to bring about results through what we might call non-action – as, for example, when through keeping still the sage makes the muddied water clear. 'Non-action' is a central concept in Daoism. However, the Chinese term is *wu-wei* and the translation 'non-action' doesn't quite capture what is important to a Daoist. The emphasis in Daoist thought is that in doing nothing one might actually be bringing something about. While standing still may in a sense be doing nothing, it is bringing about the result that the water becomes clear. A rather more accurate translation of *wu-wei* might then be 'activity that does not disrupt the natural way of things'.

This interpretation of *wu-wei* coheres with another aspect of the *Daodejing* that would be puzzling if we simply focused on the idea of passive non-action. Many of the poems in the text concern statecraft – they are about the best way to rule. This was a particularly important issue in classical China and, like other thinkers active during the Warring States Period, Daoists had a distinctive approach to this topic. The core of their approach lies in their account of leadership and is found in chapter 17:

> The greatest of rulers is but a shadowy presence;
> ... [They] are cautious and honor words.

> When their task is done and work complete,
> Their people all say, 'This is just how we are'.
>
> (Ivanhoe's translation, *Readings* 2005)

In keeping with this, chapter 60 contains the observation that '[r]uling a state is like cooking a small fish' – meaning that too much activity and fiddling will cause the fish and the state to fall apart. The ideal Daoist ruler, then, governs through the practice of *wu-wei*. If he is successful, his subjects will hardly be aware that he is there.

It is their concern with questions about leadership and governance that distinguishes thinkers in the second phase of philosophical Daoism from those, such as Yang Zhu, who represent the first stage. Yang Zhu thought that politics and authenticity were practical contradictions; the *Daodejing* attempted to demonstrate how one could live authentically in harmony with the Dao and yet engage in politics. We will now see how these various concerns are reconfigured in the next phase of Daoism's evolution.

WAYS OF BEING

Zhuangzi (Chuang Tzu *c.*369–286 BCE) is representative of the third stage in the evolution of philosophical Daoism. He is an enigmatic figure in the historical record, as nothing is known about him with any certainty except that he was a hermit whose ideas nevertheless were well known even during his lifetime. There is also evidence that he was a friend of Hui Shi (one of the philosophers of the School of Names who is discussed in the following chapter). The earliest version of the book eponymously entitled the *Zhuangzi* dates from about 300 CE and, being the product of multiple authors, does not give us uniformly reliable information about Zhuangzi's life or his thought. Nevertheless, the chapters that are most representative of the third stage of the evolution of Daoism are generally taken to have been written by Zhuangzi himself. These are referred to as the 'Inner Chapters' and comprise chapters 1–7.

Zhuangzi's thought has been described by one commentator as the 'philosophical counterpart to fireworks' (Kupperman 2001: 127). His style could not be further removed from that of his contemporary Mengzi. Chapter 1 of the *Zhuangzi* begins like this:

> There is a fish in the Northern Oblivion named Kun, and this Kun is quite huge, spanning who knows how many thousands of miles. He transforms into a bird named Peng, and this Peng has quite a back on him, stretching who knows how many thousands of miles. When he rouses himself and soars into the air, his wings are like clouds draped across the heavens. The oceans start to churn, and this bird begins his journey towards the Southern Oblivion. The Southern Oblivion – that is the Pool of Heaven.
> (Ziporyn's 2009 translation)

This fable is developed in the rest of the chapter and the audience turns out to be a cicada and a dove. Is this philosophy? Can we take it seriously? Despite its playful form, Zhuangzi is raising some weighty philosophical points.

The most basic point is that there are many different kinds of beings in the world. Some are very large, like yaks, and some are very small, like tiny birds. Some of these beings live for a long time; whereas the lifespan of others is brief. Zhuangzi noted that the perspective on the world which each of these beings has will be limited by the kind of being that it is, and he employs the example of a frog living in a well to make this point. The frog believes that the sky is just the small space it sees above it that is framed by the edges of the well. If a bird that actually flew in the immense sky were to tell the frog about its experience of the sky, the frog would regard the bird as crazy.

As Zhuangzi asks: 'And the blue on blue of the sky – is that the sky's true color? Or is it just the vast distance, going on and on without end, that looks that way?' (Ziporyn 2009: 3f.). Thinking about colour might help us to get the hang of Zhuangzi's idea. It is well known that people perceive colours in different ways. Two people might look at the same object, at the same time, and in the same lighting conditions, yet one of them might see the object as green while the other sees it as grey. Who is to say which of them, if either, is seeing the colour correctly?

The moral of Zhuangzi's stories is that different perspectives on reality are possible. Moreover, we shouldn't expect to be able to identify one perspective as superior to another because the various perspectives may all be correct from the point of view of the individuals who possess them. So we shouldn't assume that there is an absolute truth about anything, in the sense of a truth that is independent of any particular perspective. Moreover, the perspective of one kind of being might be quite useless to another kind of being. What use would the frog have for the perspective of the large bird?

Nevertheless, Zhuangzi does not seem to be claiming that all perspectives actually are equally valuable. The cicada, the frog and the dove have very narrow perspectives. Consequently, they appear quite foolish when, from their limited points of view, they try to judge the perspectives of beings with a wider range of abilities than they have. It seems that Zhuangzi is criticizing philosophers – such as Confucians and Mohists – who don't realize that their perspective is only one of many, and a limited one at that. A more valuable perspective, he suggests, would be one that realized its own limitations and refrained from making foolish and presumptuous judgements about the perspectives of others.

In choosing to communicate his ideas through fables and stories Zhuangzi is making a statement about the inadequacies he finds in the strategies of philosophical argumentation employed by his peers. He is deeply sceptical that philosophical argument can convince people to accept conclusions that they don't already agree with. Does winning an argument make the winner's view right and the loser's view wrong? Of course not, as he rightly points out. The argument may be won because the person on the winning side is more skilful at presenting her points and she may successfully argue for a conclusion that is not in fact true. Consider a short section from chapter 2 of the *Zhuangzi*:

> Saying is not just blowing. Saying says something. But if what it says is not fixed, then does it really say anything? Or does it say nothing? We think it is different from the peeping of fledglings. But is there really any difference or isn't there? How is the Way obscured that there are true and false? How are words obscured that there are *shi*, 'right,' and *fei*, 'wrong'? Where can you go that the Way does not exist? How can words exist and not be okay? The Way is obscured by small completions. Words are obscured by glory and show. So we have the rights and wrongs of the Confucians and the Mohists. Each calls right what the other calls wrong and each calls wrong what the other calls right. But if you want to right their wrongs and wrong their rights, it's better to throw them open to the light.

> There is nothing that cannot be looked at that way.
> There is nothing that cannot be looked at this way.
> But that is not the way I see things;
> Only as I know things myself do I know them.
>
> (Kjellberg's translation in Ivanhoe and Van Norden 2001: 212)

Using the terminology of modern western philosophy, we might say that Zhuangzi was a metaphysical **anti-realist**: he denied that there was one true description of reality, affirming instead that reality could be correctly described in any number of different and possibly mutually contradictory ways.

A modern commentator has schematized Zhuangzi's main argument into the following three premises and conclusion:

> 1 Whatever truth about something we think we have reached, alternative perspectives (yielding different results) are available.
> 2 We cannot rule out the possibility that one of these perspectives is superior to ours.
> 3 Even if we have good reason to reject the suggestion that any currently available perspective is superior to ours, we cannot rule out the possibility that a superior one will become available.
> 4 Therefore we can never be in a position to claim a final, optimal version of truth about anything.
>
> (Kupperman 2001: 127)

But Zhuangzi didn't just hold these views about the connection between perspectives and reality. He also thought that there was a similarly complex relation between reality and the plurality of ways in which it might be experienced. Take, for example, an ancient tree. Zhuangzi might have said that there are as many ways of experiencing this tree as there are kinds of beings and even if we only considered human beings, there might be as many different ways of experiencing the tree as there are people. Consider: How would a logger experience the tree? And what about an artist or a tree-hugger? Zhuangzi would have claimed that there is just no such thing as the definitive experience of anything. No one can claim that his or her experience is ultimately more accurate or closer to reality than anyone else's.

Given that Zhuangzi held these beliefs about the multifaceted relationship between perspectives, reality and experience, it is less surprising that he eschewed serious philosophical essays, preferring instead to write fables and perplexing stories. By means of these literary devices, Zhuangzi sought to encourage his readers to get in touch with their individual and unique way of experiencing reality.

EXEMPLARY PERSONS

Zhuangzi's advice, then, is that each one of us should live in a way that is true to the perspective and experience uniquely available to us. Such a way of living is exemplified in the story of Cook Ding, an exceptionally skilful butcher.

> The cook was carving up an ox for King Hui of Liang. Wherever his hand smacked it, wherever his shoulder leaned into it, wherever his foot braced it, wherever his knee pressed it, the thwacking tones of flesh falling from bone would echo, the knife would whiz through with its resonant thwing, each stroke ringing out the perfect note, attuned to the 'Dance of the Mulberry Grove' or the 'Jingshou Chorus' of the ancient sage-kings.
>
> (*Zhuangzi*, chapter 3; Ziporyn's 2009 translation)

Cook Ding lives up to Zhuangzi's ideal while carrying out a useful profession in life. He is so skilful at his task that it is as if he were dancing, and in his work he is guided by his ability to experience the Dao. This is a sort of mysticism that involves intense focus on the everyday details of life and the demands of one's profession. In giving us this gritty example, Zhuangzi aligns himself with the other thinkers considered in this chapter who valued knowing how to do something more than the abstract scholarly knowledge ('knowing that') which Confucians held in such high regard.

Zhuangzi suggests that it is possible to live and carry out all one's activities with the same skill that Cook Ding demonstrates in cutting meat. The whole of life can be seen as a task which one can carry out in virtuoso fashion by keeping in touch with one's experience of the Dao. What is required for this is not scholarship but knowing how to live a life attuned to the Way. Zhuangzi realized that if the Dao is really present within everything, then one should be able to experience it through experiencing individual objects, even quite humble objects like flowers and jugs. On this view, experience of the Dao isn't an experience of some other-worldly entity, as mystical experiences in western culture are sometimes thought to be. Experience of the Dao is available in our dealings with ordinary objects and through carrying out everyday tasks – cutting meat, for example.

But Zhuangzi believed that many people never access this experience of the Dao and so do not live satisfying lives. He put the blame for this on the Confucian emphasis on ritual propriety and conventional social traditions. Like the other thinkers considered in this chapter, he was convinced that people were following artificial patterns of behaviour laid down by tradition and that this prevented them from having an authentic experience of the Dao. Traditional morality and social mores prescribed to a person what he or she ought to feel and do in any given situation. Living according to these conventions was, according to Zhuangzi, to be radically out of touch both with one's true nature and with the Way.

Given what has been said above, you might expect Zhuangzi to have advocated that everyone should stop acting according to conventional morality and simply do whatever takes his or her fancy, regardless of whether this includes things that conventional morality regards as very bad, such as rape and murder. But Zhuangzi's view is more subtle than this because he has not simply told us to abandon conventions and morality, but to do so in order that we might live in ways that are attuned to the Dao. Part of what this means is that we should live in harmony with the rest of the world, and this entails living in harmony with other people. Such harmony would be disrupted by acts of violence and hence these have no place in Zhuangzi's proposal.

Living in harmony with the world was taken to include being in harmony with your emotions (as these are, after all, part of nature). This does not mean that a person should be at the mercy of his or her emotions; rather they should be in control of them. There is an example of this in the *Zhuangzi*, although it is not from the 'Inner Chapters' so is probably the work of a follower of Zhuangzi. Chapter 18 relates how a friend visited Zhuangzi shortly after the death of Zhuangzi's wife. The friend found Zhuangzi behaving in what seemed to be a highly inappropriate way: beating on a tub and singing! When questioned, Zhuangzi explained that he had been upset at first but had then realized that there was no cause for distress because all that had happened was a change of state, like that from summer to autumn. It is natural that things change and it would be foolishness to be upset.

The message here resonates with the core teaching of Buddhism. Namely, everything is impermanent so don't become too attached to the things of this world, not even to the people one loves. One should never be so attached to something or someone that one's inner peace is lost or one's emotional stability is unbalanced. To help us to achieve this state of detachment towards things, Zhuangzi suggested that we consider the idea that the importance which things have for us is relative to our perspective. Changing our perspective might then result in a re-evaluation of what is important (two stories in chapter 2 of the *Zhuangzi* illustrate this: the story of the monkeys and the famous account of Zhuangzi dreaming of being a butterfly). If we see things in a different light we might notice that what previously seemed very important actually doesn't matter. Another technique Zhuangzi recommended to train ourselves in detachment involves what can be translated as 'fasting of the heart' – focusing our concentration inward in order to become attuned to the deep nature of things (see *Zhuangzi*, chapter 4).

So far in this chapter we have considered different answers given by thinkers who were all later categorized as 'Daoists' to the fundamental questions: 'How to live an authentic life?' and 'What is the best way to preserve life and avoid injury?'. Zhuangzi gave philosophical Daoism's final answer to these questions. He answered the first question by advising us to seek to experience the Dao through whatever we are doing – there is no need to avoid society, we can be butchers or bakers or candlestick makers, as long as we know how to live and act according to the Way. His answer to the second question is that we must try to develop the perspective from which we can see that there is no real difference between life and death. Life is only life from a certain point of view, and death is only death from a certain point of view – so our conventional negative thoughts about death must be rejected. Death is part of the balance of nature and as such is neither good nor bad; it simply is and the sage should regard it with equanimity. So the questions that puzzled Yang Zhu about how to preserve life and avoid injury are no longer important.

LEGALISM

The ideas considered above about the possibility of an authentic life centred on the Dao had lasting popularity, not least because they offered a way to live with integrity in the troubled and unpredictable political and social conditions prevalent in China towards the end of the Warring States Period. But other currents were also at work in the sea of ideas that formed the intellectual world of the day. Amongst these was a movement called Legalism whose main representative was Han Feizi (*c.*280–233 BCE). It is appropriate to consider this final thinker at the close of this chapter because his thought draws on elements of the various philosophies already considered in this chapter and the previous one and synthesizes them into a new configuration.

Han Feizi was educated in the Confucian tradition and was a student of Xunxi (see Chapter 4). Like Xunzi – and Yang Zhu – he held that human nature is self-interested, but he disagreed with him about what should be done in the light of this unfortunate fact. Han Feizi's proposal is more akin to Mozi's than to Xunxi's in that it emphasizes the role of rewards and punishments in shaping behaviour rather than the role of tradition, learning and the rites (see the eponymous *Han Feizi*, in *Readings*, chapter 7).

Rejection of tradition is one aspect of Han Feizi's thought that seems particularly modern. Arguing that there is no reason to accept that what worked in the past would work today, he proposed that the troubles of the times called for a new solution. The solution he came up with was bureaucracy (something which in the West is thought of as quintessentially modern, but in China is over 2,000 years old). Through the bureaucratic administration of rewards and punishments, the system of government he designed made it practically impossible for people to act from self-interest without simultaneously acting in the public interest. In this system the ruler would have nothing to do as the bureaucratic machine would take care of everything. Han Feizi effectively borrowed from the discussion of statecraft in the *Daodejing* to recommend this idea to his contemporaries. He advocated that the ruler remain 'still' and not reveal his intentions to his underlings. Ruling will take place through 'non-action' so that the 'ministers will be anxious and fearful' (*Readings*: 196).

As a result of political intrigue, just twelve years before the unification of China finally ended the Warring States Period in 221 BCE, Han Feizi committed suicide, rather than be executed by the state. The ruler of Qin, who had ordered his execution, later declared himself to be First Emperor, although he only managed to hold power until 207 BCE. The short time of the Qin dynasty was momentous for Chinese intellectual history and it brought the classical era to a decisive close. The same official who had plotted the downfall of Han Feizi was the mastermind of a far-reaching programme of book burning which targeted philosophy books for destruction. In a shocking implementation of the advice of the *Daodejing*, the people were to be kept away from learning. Many philosophical schools (such as Mohism) disappeared, but those versions of the Way that survived and were promoted by organized movements had laid solid foundations. These were developed by the commentarial traditions which took centre stage at this point. It was through the work of the commentators that 'Daoism' came to be regarded as a distinct movement like 'Confucianism'.

SUMMARY OF CHAPTER 5

This chapter has introduced the main concepts of Daoist philosophy by explaining the different ways Yang Zhu, 'Laozi', and Zhuangzi answered the two key questions: 'How to live an authentic life?' and 'What is the best way to preserve life and avoid injury?'. In doing so it has portrayed Daoism as proposing conceptions of the Way that rivalled others views available at the time.

Egoism was the first theory to be addressed as this was a hallmark of the earliest form of Daoist thought. Yang Zhu's position was considered and contrasted with the ethical views of Confucians and Mohists. The early Daoists believed that both the Confucians and the Mohists were mistaken in their belief that a well-lived life was one that took place in the midst of social relationships. Instead they emphasized that to live authentically requires that one's life be in harmony with the Dao, and that such a life can only be enjoyed in retreat from society. This discussion raised the question of what the

Dao is. To answer this we turned to the *Daodejing* and considered different aspects of the Daoist idea that the good life is one that is vitally connected with the Dao. A contrast was made between the Daoist ideal of spontaneous action in accordance with the Dao and, what Daoists would disparagingly regard as, tradition-bound Confucian moral calculation.

We saw that Daoists accused Confucians of bringing vice into the world as a result of their notion of virtue. This was one example of the recurrent theme within Daoist philosophy that opposites produce each other. The view that virtue produces vice provided a perspective to explain the importance of non-action (*wu-wei*) in Daoist thought. The sage has mastered the art of non-action, as exemplified by the story of Cook Ding in the *Zhuangzi*. Another feature of the sage is equanimity, and we considered this by reviewing Zhuangzi's ideas about the relativity of what appears to be important to us. We saw how Zhuangzi turned Daoist philosophy in a metaphysical direction as he considered the nature of things and their relationship with the mind, language and experience. These topics are considered further in the following chapter.

REFERENCES AND FURTHER READING

PRIMARY TEXTS

Key sections of the main primary texts discussed in this chapter (the *Daodejing*, the *Zhuangzi* and the *Han Feizi*) are in Philip J. Ivanhoe and Bryan W. Van Norden, *Readings in Classical Chinese Philosophy*, 2nd edition (Indianapolis: Hackett, 2005). See also the 1st edition for some of the passages cited in this chapter.

Wing-tsit Chan (ed.), *A Sourcebook in Chinese Philosophy*, 4th edition (Princeton: Princeton University Press, 1973).

Yu-lan Fung, *A Short History of Chinese Philosophy: A Systematic Account of Chinese Thought from Its Origin to the Present Day* (New York: The Free Press, 1976).

Angus C. Graham, trans., *Chang-tzu: The Inner Chapters* (Indianapolis: Hackett, 2001). Reprint. An interpretive translation of the core chapters of the *Zhuangzi*.

Also see D. C. Lau's translation, *Tao Te Ching* (New York: Penguin, 1963). This is based on the traditional version of the text and can be compared to the more recent translation by Victor M. Mair, *Tao Te Ching* (New York: Bantam Books, 1990), which relies on the version of the text discovered at the archaeological site of Mawangdui in the 1970s.

For the most significant writings of Zhuangzi and a selection from the traditional commentaries on his work see *Zhuangzi: The Essential Writings*, translated by Brook Ziporyn (Indianapolis: Hackett, 2009).

Thomas Cleary's translation of the *Daodejing*, and other Daoist texts, is in *The Taoist Classics: The Collected Translations of Thomas Cleary*, volume 1 (Boston: Shambhala, 2003).

SECONDARY LITERATURE

Mark Csikszentmihalyi and Philip J. Ivanhoe (eds), *Essays on the Religious and Philosophical Aspects of the Laozi* (Albany: SUNY Press, 1999).

Angus C. Graham, *Disputers of the Tao* (Chicago: Open Court, 1989).

Chad Hansen, *A Daoist Theory of Chinese Thought* (New York: OUP, 1992), part II, 1.5.2.

Paul Kjellberg and Philip J. Ivanhoe (eds), *Essays on Skepticism, Relativism and Ethics in the* Zhuangzi (Albany: SUNY Press, 1996).

Joel J. Kupperman, *Classic Asian Philosophy: A Guide to the Essential Texts* (Oxford: OUP, 2001).

JeeLoo Liu, *An Introduction to Chinese Philosophy* (Oxford: Blackwell, 2006), chapters 6, 7 and 8.

James Miller, *Daoism: A Short Introduction* (Oxford: Oneworld, 2005).

Hans-Georg Moeller, *Daoism Explained: From the Dream of the Butterfly to the Fishnet Allegory* (Chicago and La Salle, IL: Open Court, 2004).

Edward Slingerland, *Effortless Action: Wu-Wei as Conceptual Metaphor and Spiritual Ideal in Early China* (Oxford: OUP, 2003).

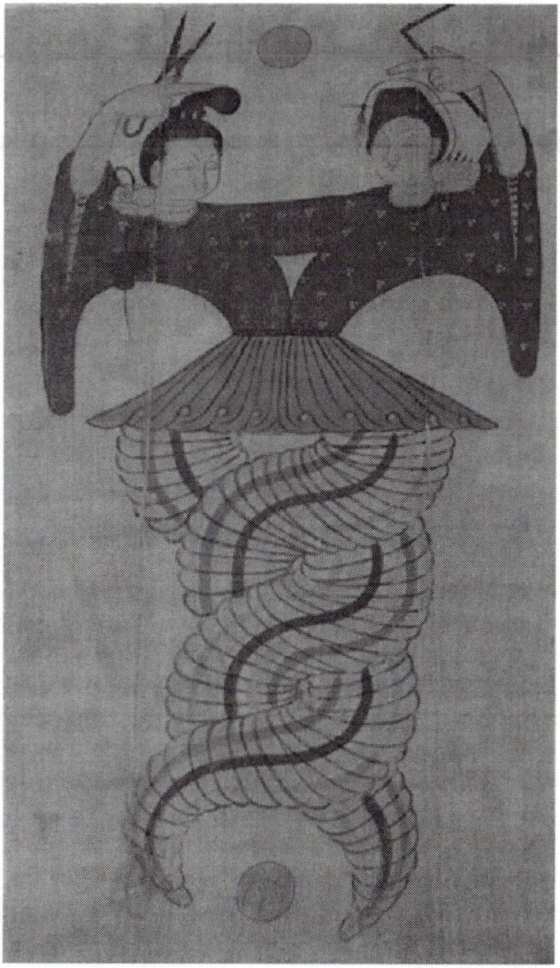

Figure 5.2 A mid-eighth-century painting, on silk, depicting Fu Xi and Nuwa. According to Chinese legend, this husband and wife were the first and second sovereigns of China and played a key role in the introduction of civilization. Fu Xi is credited with the earliest sections of the *Yijing*. The intertwined serpents are in the caduceus form which was a motif found in both Bronze Age Mesopotamia and in the Indus Valley culture. This eighth-century work testifies to the creative interaction and synthesis of Chinese and Indian culture that matured during the Tang dynasty. On the cultural significance of the caduceus form see McEvilley 2002: chapter 8.

6

MIND

The account of the philosophies of China presented in the last two chapters is taken up again here as we turn to some major developments that took place after the classical era. The core ideas of neo-Confucian philosophy are introduced as we consider the relationship between that philosophy and ideas from the School of Names, Daoism and the emergent Chinese Buddhist philosophy. Two key questions are addressed: 'How are words and things related?' and 'How is the mind related to the world?'.

Thinkers connected with the School of Names laid the conceptual groundwork for many of the ideas to be examined in this chapter. Hence, although this takes us briefly back into the classical era, we begin with a discussion of this school.

WORDS AND THINGS

Despite its title, the 'School of Names' (*Ming-jia/Ming chia*) was never a school of thought in the way that Confucianism or Mohism were. Instead, during the Han dynasty the term came to be applied retrospectively to group together a number of thinkers active in the late fourth and early third centuries BCE who shared a love of rigorous argumentation and paradox. While this style of philosophizing was no longer popular by the time of the Han its influence on later philosophical movements was significant.

Some explanation is required of why this analytic trend in Chinese philosophy that was exemplified by the School of Names disappeared. The short story is that it was a victim of its own success. Philosophers associated with the School of Names became adepts at developing logical paradoxes and showing how arguments could be used with equal success to defend both sides in a disagreement (the earliest figure associated with them, Deng Xi, appears to have been a lawyer). The effect of this was to precipitate a crisis of confidence in the powers of rational argumentation and to generate deep scepticism about the ability of language to express anything non-relative. Despite the notable efforts of later Mohists, this led Confucians and Daoists to shun formal logical tools and to prefer alternative intellectual strategies, focusing their efforts instead on the use of analogy and illustration and the development of commentarial traditions. As we shall see, the much later emergence of neo-Confucian philosophy was significant because it signalled a move away from reliance on commentary and allowed more scope for systematic thinking and the exploration of original ideas.

In Chapter 4, we observed that Kongzi was interested in the correct use of words (see *Analects* 13.13), although there is no record of him having developed an elaborate theory on this topic. Philosophers associated with the School of Names took up this interest in words and quickly realized that a number of philosophical puzzles could be generated by thinking about the relationship between words and things.

Two philosophers are especially significant in this respect: Hui Shi (Hui Shih, *c.*380–305 BCE) and Gongsun Long (Kung-sun Lung, born *c.*380 BCE). Unfortunately the details of Hui Shi's arguments have been lost and only a list of the ten theses he defended remains to give us a flavour of his views (for a discussion of these ten theses see Van Norden 2011: 103–7). Consider, for instance, his ninth thesis: 'I know the center of the world: it is north of Yan and south of Yue' (paraphrased in ibid., p. 104). The thesis might not seem puzzling unless you know that Yan was a state in the far north and Yue was a state in the far south. The point was that where the centre of the world is located depends on where one is positioned; there is no absolute centre. Hui Shi also puzzled his contemporaries with his seventh thesis: 'I left for Yue today but arrived yesterday' (ibid.). This thesis suggests that whatever the terms 'yesterday' and 'today' refer to must be relative; indeed, everyday is today at some point in time but it is also yesterday at some other point. I'm writing this paragraph today, but tomorrow I will have written it yesterday. There are ongoing debates about how best to interpret Hui Shi's ideas, but the thrust of his theses can be summarized in the claim (which clearly influenced his friend Zhuangzi) that actual things are relative.

In contrast to Hui Shi's preoccupation with the relativity of things, Gongsun Long emphasized the non-relativity, or absoluteness, that he took to be presupposed by our use of certain words. To see what he meant let us consider dogs (although he preferred horses). His argument does not concern the fact that we can use different words to refer to dogs as a class (such as *Hund* if we are speaking German or *chien* if we are French). Nor does it concern the proper names of individual dogs; my dog is called Jackson and yours might be called Tiepolo. Hui Shi might have noted that individual dogs change over time from birth to death – Jackson's muzzle is greyer now than it was three years ago – and he might have concluded that individual dogs are relative. He might even have supported his claim with the observation that 'the dog is young' and 'the dog is old' can both be true of the same dog (whether Jackson is young or old depends both on when we evaluate him and on what we compare him with – he might be young compared with a long-lived turtle and old compared with a short-lived butterfly). Gongsun Long would not dispute any of this, but he would still claim that there is something non-relative about dogs. This non-relative thing is what all dogs share, possession of which makes them dogs and not something else: we shall call it Dog-nature. Every individual dog possesses this for as long as it lives. But the fact that it possesses it, or ceases to possess it, does not change the Dog-nature itself because that is absolute and thereby unaffected by how many individual dogs come into or go out of existence. A word like 'dog' is a common term that denotes a class of particular things by identifying the common attribute – in this case Dog-nature – that makes them all members of that class. The word 'dog' (or its equivalents within other languages) then points us beyond particular dogs to the universal Dog-nature that they all share (see Fung 1976: 90).

This underlying universal nature which makes things what they are is what Gongsun Long seeks to draw our attention to by claiming that certain words refer to something absolute. So now combining these two views, we can say with Hui Shi that actual things (e.g. individual dogs) are changeable and relative, and with Gongsun Long we can say that the universals (e.g. Dog-nature) that are denoted by certain words are unchanging and therefore absolute.

INDIVIDUALS AND UNIVERSALS

As a result of these reflections, a distinction between that which 'lies within shapes and features' and that which 'lies beyond shapes and features' was introduced into Chinese philosophy and it became hugely important (see Fung 1976: 91). That which lies within shapes and features is the actual: individual things possessing qualities such as colour, texture and weight. But what lies beyond shapes and features? The universals noted by Gongsun Long lie beyond shapes and features; and these cannot be experienced, because they are completely lacking in particular qualities. One can experience an individual dog by perceiving its colour, shape, texture and, perhaps, hearing its bark, but one cannot experience the universal Dog-nature. Moreover, it is not accidental that we cannot experience universals. It is in principle impossible to experience them because they do not possess any of the qualities which we could ever experience (we might say that possession of any of these qualities would entail that something was an actual individual thing and not a universal). Shortly we will see how the distinction between individuals and universals was absorbed into neo-Confucian philosophy.

But before discussing neo-Confucianism, we next turn to another philosophical tradition without an encounter with which Confucianism's intellectual history would have surely followed a very different trajectory.

EMPTINESS AND INSIGHT

Several different forms of Chinese Buddhist philosophy evolved once Buddhism took root in China. Our focus here is on a form of Buddhism called Chan because this was both the one most permeated by the Sinitic intellectual milieu that preceded it and the most influential on the non-Buddhist traditions that took shape after it. (For a discussion of Chan and three other Chinese Buddhist schools see J. Liu 2006: part II.) Moreover, Chan was the only school of Chinese Buddhist philosophy to outlast the Tang dynasty (618–906 CE).

The word 'Chan' is a Chinese rendition of the Sanskrit term '*dhyana*', which in English means meditation. The Japanese word for 'Chan' is 'Zen' and this is the term most familiar in the West. As a unique fusion of philosophical Daoism and Indian Buddhism, Chan was a genuinely new form of Buddhism that was shaped by the Chinese context from which it emerged. Before exploring Chan more deeply, however, we need to prepare the ground by looking at what led up to it.

APPROPRIATION AND ASSIMILATION

There isn't a definite answer to the question of when Buddhism arrived in China, although it is certain that by 150 CE it was well known there. Most scholars agree that Buddhism came to China during the Han dynasty.

Buddhism had always been a missionary religion and its message was spread by bands of itinerant monks. When it first entered China, sources suggest that it aroused popular distaste because of its negative attitude to the family. As we have seen, in classical China the family was widely regarded as the core social unit upon which the well-being of individuals and the state ultimately depended. It is not surprising that many Chinese found the Buddhist ideal of celibacy extremely unattractive. Buddhists told people that they should leave their families to pursue the spiritual ideal of *nirvāṇa*. Nothing had prepared the Chinese of the classical era for this. Even Daoism which, as noted above, began by advocating retreat from the world, had arrived at Zhuangzi's claim that the ultimately fulfilling experience of the Dao was available to everyone without their having to renounce their ordinary activities and family life.

Largely because of this major cultural difference, Buddhism struck many Chinese as an alien, barbarian religion. Although some Chinese did adopt Buddhism the early converts tended to be from the lower strata of society. This gave the upper-class, educated Chinese further reason to find Buddhism unappealing – it was perceived as a religion of farmers and menial workers.

The transmission of Buddhism from India to China was further complicated by the fact that many distinct schools of Buddhism already existed in India by the time Buddhism began to penetrate East Asia. Each of these schools claimed to represent the historical Buddha's teaching authentically. Moreover, in India during the Han dynasty Buddhism was going through some quite dramatic changes. By the Common Era, the surviving Buddhist schools could be grouped into two major streams: Theravāda and Mahāyāna (see Cantwell 2010: chapter 5). The monks that entered China spreading Buddhism came from both streams, with the result that they were not all saying the same thing! The Mahāyānins proclaimed an ideal of universal salvation and taught that the universe consisted of several world systems each with its own Buddha. Theravādins, by contrast, understood the world as a single system in which it was up to each individual to achieve *nirvāṇa*. To add to the confusion caused by this, Mahāyāna Buddhism itself arrived in China in various forms.

The Chinese recipients of these conflicting accounts of the Buddha's teachings attempted to deal with the inconsistency by means of the idea that the historical Buddha had given his teaching in different stages. The Theravādin teachings were the first stage, and the Mahāyānin teachings the final stage. In this way it was possible to hold that each stream of Buddhist tradition was in possession of authentic teachings stemming from the mouth of the historical Buddha, with the qualification that the Mahāyānins had the latest, most complete version. This theory accounted for the otherwise puzzling differences between the versions of Buddhism promoted by the two different sets of monks. Understanding it helps us to make sense of the transformations that Buddhism underwent after its arrival in China, because Chinese forms of Buddhism drew deeply from both of these major Indian Buddhist streams – but most especially from Mahāyāna traditions.

The assimilation of Indian Buddhism into China occurred in four stages (see Wright 1959):

Stage 1: The Period of Preparation (*c.*65–317 CE).
Stage 2: The Period of Domestication (*c.*317–589 CE).
Stage 3: The Period of Acceptance and Independent Growth (*c.*589–900 CE).
Stage 4: The Period of Appropriation (*c.*900–1900 CE).

In the early fourth century CE, Buddhism's fortunes in China improved when members of the Chinese aristocracy began to take a serious interest in its teachings. Sophisticated Buddhist texts were translated into Chinese, thus allowing Chinese intellectuals to see that there was more to Buddhism than many of them had previously judged. However, many Chinese scholars seem to have thought Buddhism to be a foreign version of philosophical Daoism. Consequently, when they translated Buddhist texts it seemed quite natural to them to use the Daoist terminology with which they and their readers were familiar. The eventual result of this practice was a form of Chinese Buddhism which had a huge intellectual debt to Daoism. But the Daoization of Buddhism did facilitate Buddhism's eventual full acceptance into China.

The growing appreciation and gradual acceptance of Buddhism in China culminated during the Tang dynasty. It was during this time that Buddhism began to have a huge impact on Chinese culture and intellectual life, even receiving imperial patronage. From this time on Buddhism can legitimately be regarded as the third of China's religious and philosophical systems, alongside Confucianism and Daoism.

Although Chan is first recognizable during the Tang dynasty, it had important intellectual and cultural antecedents in the thought of earlier Chinese Buddhists. It is neither possible nor necessary here to go into detail about these earlier thinkers, but a few remarks will suffice to explain the relationship between their approach to Buddhism and what came later.

PRECURSORS TO CHAN

The earliest Buddhist philosophers in China were particularly influenced by a strand of Indian Mahāyāna Buddhism which taught that within all sentient beings there is a Buddha-nature. The origins of this idea are not well understood, although it is found in an Indian text (the *Ratnagotravibhāga*) which may date from the mid-third century CE. The text distinguishes between the Buddha-nature as it exists in a hidden or obscure form (which it names *tathāgatagarba*) and the Buddha-nature in an unobscured form (which it names *dharmakāya*). Although *tathāgatagarba* and *dharmakāya* were thought to be one and the same ultimate reality, the claim was that until we are enlightened we are not able to apprehend their identity. Early

Chinese Buddhists were taught that although each one of us is endowed with the Buddha-nature only those who are enlightened have come to an awareness of this.

By the sixth century CE, under the influence of Yogācāra and, especially, Cittamātra 'Mind Only' ideas (see Chapter 2, above) imported from India, the Buddha-nature had come to be interpreted as consciousness. *Tathāgatagarba* was regarded as impure consciousness that is somehow limited – or defiled – by being embedded in the phenomenal world of our experience. *Dharmakāya*, on the other hand, was thought to be pure consciousness without 'defilements', limitations, or distinctions. In short, pure consciousness (i.e. the Buddha-nature as *dharmakāya*) was understood to be a singular unchanging reality forming the essence of all that exists. This view was promoted by the *Lankavatara Sūtra*, at the core of which is the so-called Universal Mind, or Mind Only, interpretation of the Buddha-nature. (See Williams 1989: chapter 5.)

However, the idea of a universal Buddha-nature was not alone in exerting a deep impact on early Chinese Buddhists. The perspective of Nāgārjuna's Madhyamaka School (see Chapters 2 and 3) was also influential. Nāgārjuna advocated the methodological principle of denying all positive statements and then denying the denial. One might say, for example: '*X*', then 'not-*X*', then 'not-not-*X*'. This process was designed to leave one speechless having gone beyond assertion and denial. The approach must have resonated with many early Chinese followers of Buddhism as it has striking similarities to the theory of Zhuangzi (see Chapter 5). You'll recall that Zhuangzi recommended that the good Daoist should arrive at a state of 'fasting of the heart' – having forgotten the apparent distinctions between things. Nāgārjuna's method of denial followed by denial of the denial seemed to lead one to the kind of state recommended by Zhuangzi because following the approach prescribed by either would render one unable reliably to apply concepts to things.

Early Chinese Buddhists combined a Madhyamaka perspective with an understanding of the Buddha-nature, and fused these with certain Daoist convictions. They took the teaching that humans are endowed with the same Buddha-nature to imply that all of us are spiritual equals in so far as the only difference between a Buddha (or a sage) and an unenlightened person is that the former is aware of their true nature and the latter is not. Some then proposed that each of us could realize the Buddha-nature through the process recommended by Nāgārjuna. The realization of one's Buddha-nature would, they thought, be instantaneous. It would be achieved in a moment of enlightenment rather than through years of patient study and monastic discipline. Applying the Daoist idea of *wu-wei* (see Chapter 5), they argued that trying to achieve enlightenment was futile. Instead, one simply had to realize that one was already enlightened. (In fact, being enlightened is to have realized this – so don't worry if what it means to 'realize' it isn't transparent to you!) These ideas later became central to Chan philosophy – to which we now turn.

DEVELOPMENT AND EVOLUTION OF CHAN

An Indian monk named Bodhidharma is traditionally regarded as the founder of Chan Buddhism; he is said to have arrived in China from India in 520 CE. Centuries later followers of Chan would argue that the historical Buddha had not only given the teaching which had been passed down through the Buddhist Sūtras but also had passed on a secret teaching. This esoteric teaching had never been written down and was transmitted from teacher to disciple by word of mouth until Bodhidharma received it from his teacher and brought it to China. Bodhidharma was thought to have been twenty-eighth in the line of those who had received the Buddha's esoteric message. Scholars disagree about whether or not Bodhidharma was a historical figure (speculative dates for his life are 470–534 CE). Despite this uncertainty, to this day many regard him as the First Patriarch of Chan Buddhism. He is thought to have passed on the Buddha's esoteric teaching to an appointed successor, the Second Patriarch, who passed it on to the Third Patriarch, and so on.

The Fifth Patriarch, Hongren (Hung-jen, 601–74 CE), is the first patriarch of whom we have definite historical records. His patriarchate took place during the early part of the Tang dynasty. Hongren had two outstanding disciples who were rivals for the position of Sixth Patriarch. These two were Shenxiu (Shen-hsiu, *c.*606–706) and Huineng (638–713). The rivalry between them caused Chan Buddhism to split into two separate and antagonistic schools. Shenxiu became the founder of the Northern School and Huineng became the founder of the Southern School. At first the Northern School was the most successful and for a time Shenxiu was regarded as the rightful Sixth Patriarch. However, the Southern School quickly superseded the Northern School, leading to Huineng being regarded as the Sixth Patriarch (although the Southern School's success probably did not occur during Huineng's lifetime). Many scholars now suspect that it was Huineng's disciple Shenhui (670–762) who was responsible for the success of the Southern School. Anyway, it is clear that the key later developments in Chan Buddhism were inspired by the teachings of Huineng's Southern School.

The disagreement between Shenxiu and Huineng stemmed from a fundamental difference in their philosophical views that was the result of their each emphasizing a different aspect of earlier Buddhist thought. Drawing on the *Lankavatara Sūtra*, Shenxiu was primarily influenced by the Universal Mind interpretation of the Buddha-nature, while Huineng's interpretation of the Buddha-nature was informed by Nāgārjuna's Madhyamaka notion that all things are empty of 'own-being' (*svabhāva*). (Huineng was also influenced by another Buddhist text, the *Diamond Sūtra*.)

Chan tradition contains an account of how this difference was exposed. When Hongren, the Fifth Patriarch, sought to appoint a successor he invited his monks to write a short verse expressing the core of his teaching. Here is Shenxiu's composition:

> The body is the tree of insight;
> The mind is like a clear mirror.
> Always clean and polish it;
> Never allow dirt or dust.
>
> (Ivanhoe 2009: 15)

In the background of this poem lies a particular understanding of the Universal Mind interpretation of the Buddha-nature. Notice the prominent assumption that we must *strive* to get rid of impediments which prevent us from realizing that everything is Universal Mind and everything has the Buddha-nature.

Huineng replied to Shenxiu:

> Insight originally has no tree;
> The bright mirror has no stand.
> Buddha nature is always pure and clean;
> How could there ever be dirt or dust?
>
> (Ibid., 16)

Huineng's poem, in contrast to Shenxiu's, relies on an understanding of the Buddha-nature that is indebted to Nāgārjuna's idea that everything is fundamentally without 'own-being'. Given that there is neither body nor mind, there cannot be any impediments to realizing the Buddha-nature; the Buddha-nature is itself 'empty' or void, in Nāgārjuna's sense of lacking 'own-being'. It follows that apparent distinctions, such as that between the defiled mind of the unenlightened and the undefiled mind of the enlightened, are spurious; all reality is on exactly the same level because everything possesses the Buddha-nature to exactly the same degree. This implies that the Buddha-nature can be encountered in absolutely anything; an implication which led a later follower of the Southern School – when asked what the Buddha was – to assert that the Buddha was a dried up shit-stick! It also led to the view, which became characteristic of the Southern School, that enlightenment could be triggered suddenly by anything at all if only that thing's Buddha-nature were glimpsed.

These two poems are recorded in the *Platform Sūtra*, a work which later Chan Buddhists regarded as the foundational text of their school (for a partial translation and commentary see Ivanhoe 2009). Traditionally it was thought to have been written by Huineng and it contains an account of how the Fifth Patriarch recognized him as the true Sixth Patriarch. It also explains how the Fifth Patriarch advised him to run away lest the other monks harm him in their jealousy. It now seems likely that this story was added to the text to explain why Shenxiu was regarded as the Sixth Patriarch for many years after the death of the Fifth. The inclusion of this *ad hoc* explanation suggests that the *Platform Sūtra* was written some time after Huineng's death.

Assuming that the *Platform Sūtra* does accurately express Huineng's teaching, it shows that he developed Nāgārjuna's core claim that things have neither being nor non-being (see Chapter 3). Huineng claimed that there was an even deeper truth behind this claim. He interpreted Nāgārjuna's terms 'being' as *yu* and 'non-being' as *wu*. *Yu* was the term used by Daoists to refer to what exists, that is, what is within shapes and features, while *wu* was the Daoist term for what did not exist in this sense, that is, what was beyond shapes and features. So Nāgārjuna's core idea was interpreted using Daoist terms which subtly changed its meaning. The claim that things have neither 'being' nor 'non-being' became the claim that things are neither *wu* nor *yu*. Huineng then took the deeper truth to be that things are neither *wu* nor *yu*, and neither not-*yu* nor not-*wu*.

Huineng declared that Nāgārjuna's idea, thus reinterpreted, was the First Principle of Chan Buddhism. The hallmark of the First Principle is that it cannot be explained in terms of anything else, because then whatever had been used to explain it would be more ultimate than the First Principle. This would entail that the First Principle was not in fact the First Principle. Another consequence of this understanding of the First Principle is that it cannot be explained verbally. Echoing ideas from Zhuangzi and the School of Names, the highest level of spiritual attainment was regarded as a kind of knowing how, or knack, 'not residing in words or letters' (see Ivanhoe 2009: 7). This gave rise to a variety of unusual pedagogical practices in the later Chan tradition. For instance, a Master might try to startle a student across the threshold of enlightenment by administering a timely beating or pulling on the student's nose.

ENLIGHTENMENT

The idea that the First Principle is inexplicable was thought to follow from the claim that it has something to do with *wu*. As explained above, in the Chinese intellectual tradition the term *wu* denoted what, lacking particular qualities, was beyond shapes and features. It was taken for granted that only what was within shapes and features could be talked about because what was beyond shapes and features lacked qualities (consider – what can we really say about Dog-nature other than that all dogs are in possession of it?). Even calling the First Principle 'Mind', as the rival Northern School advocated, was unacceptable to the Southern School because this was to give a name to the nameless.

The Indian Buddhists' goal of enlightenment was thus reinterpreted by thinkers within the Southern School as the non-intellectual realization of the truth of the First Principle. Such enlightenment was thought to occur all of a sudden. There could be no gradual steps leading to the realization of the First Principle; because of its ultimate nature, one either understood it or one did not. If one didn't understand it, then study and meditation would not help. Study would not help because the First Principle was not really an intellectual principle; it confounded the intelligence in a way that Nāgārjuna would surely have approved.

Nevertheless, Chan Buddhists aimed to arrive at knowledge of the First Principle while recognizing that, because of its unusual nature, such knowledge would really be non-knowledge. The state of non-knowledge to which they aspired bears a striking resemblance to the state recommended by Zhuangzi. Thus the aim of Chan Buddhism can be seen to be a novel fusion of the aspirations of Buddhism and Daoism.

Another fusion of ideas is apparent in the method Chan Buddhists of the Southern School advocated for arriving at non-knowledge of the First Principle. Their advice was that anyone seeking enlightenment should not do anything out of the ordinary. No unusual or excessive spiritual practices were necessary. Instead, the Chan practitioner should cultivate enlightenment through non-cultivation. Trying too hard to reach enlightenment was considered counterproductive. In fact, the practice of self-cultivation through *wu-wei* was recommended! Thus this form of Buddhism assimilated another quintessentially Daoist concept.

One Chan Master, Lin Ji (Yi-hsüan, *c.*810–66), counselled that, as there is no place for deliberate effort on the path to Buddhahood, the aspirant should merely carry on with the ordinary tasks of life. His advice was to 'relieve one's bowels, pass water, wear one's clothes, eat one's meals, and when tired, lie down' (in Fung 1976: 260). Again, this is remarkably similar to the method for self-fulfilment advocated by Zhuangzi in a much earlier era. As we saw in the previous chapter, Zhuangzi deployed the example of Cook Ding to promote the view that the Dao was to be experienced through carrying out one's everyday practical activities in a natural and spontaneous manner. The Chan Masters also adopted this solution.

Once more revealing their affinity to Daoism, many Chan Masters refer to the desired sudden enlightenment (*dunwu* in Chinese, *satori* in Japanese) as 'the vision of the Dao'. As in Daoism, this vision was not something acquired gradually, but was rather the immediate result of suddenly seeing and experiencing the everyday world in an entirely different way. A student who was thought to be close to reaching this state was regarded as if he or she was poised on the edge of a precipice. Leaping into the void would bring about immediate enlightenment. A good Chan teacher was supposed to know when a student was ready to make the leap, and to be ready to help by administering one of the aforementioned beatings or nose pulls. The shock of the incongruous physical assault was meant to assist the student at this crucial point in their spiritual maturation. More subtle forms of assistance were also developed. A Master might give a student an insoluble intellectual riddle to ponder, such as: 'What is the sound of one hand clapping?'. These riddles are called *gong'an* in Chinese (*kōan* in Japanese), and they are still used by Chan practitioners today.

Sudden enlightenment is described as akin to when the bottom falls out of a tub of water in that it comes to a person when she least expects it. When it has occurred, the enlightened one finds that she does not have the answers to the questions which had previously puzzled her, but, like Zhuangzi, she realizes that these questions are no longer important.

Chan Buddhism, then, is the result of a combination of Nāgārjuna's Madhyamaka form of Mahāyāna Buddhism, an interpretation of the Buddha-nature as within all things, and the central insights of the Daoist philosopher Zhuangzi (who himself was influenced by Hui Shi of the School of Names). This combination was forged by the Sixth Patriarch Huineng and became the core teaching of the Southern School. This form of Buddhism spread outside China and struck deep roots in Japan where today there is a living tradition of Zen Buddhism taking a variety of forms, the best known of which is Rinzai Zen. Moreover, Zen is the dominant form of Buddhism practised in the United States today and its popularity there has been growing at least since the 1960s; only recently has its success been rivalled by the appeal of Tibetan Buddhism.

PRINCIPLES

Neo-Confucianism developed under the influence of Buddhism – especially that of Chan Buddhism, which, as explained above, was itself indebted to philosophical Daoism. Many of the most distinguished neo-Confucian thinkers were familiar with Buddhist metaphysics and some of them had studied with Buddhist teachers. Although it originated in the eighth century CE during the Tang dynasty, neo-Confucianism emerged as a fully matured philosophical system in the eleventh century CE during the Song dynasty

(960–1279), and it remained a key force in Chinese intellectual life until the seventeenth century. Between the end of the classical era of Chinese philosophy and the eighth century CE about a thousand years had passed. During this time exposure to Buddhist philosophy had given many Chinese intellectuals a taste for metaphysical speculation. Eventually criticism of Confucian philosophy's apparent lack of interest in metaphysical questions grew to a swell. This dissatisfaction prompted Confucian scholars to travel in new intellectual directions in their efforts to give an account of the Way of Kongzi that would be adequate to the needs of the day – the result of this was neo-Confucianism.

Neo-Confucian philosophy developed and matured between 700 and 1200 CE. It is sometimes referred to as *Dao-Xue* (Learning of the Dao). It should not be confused with 'new Confucianism' or 'contemporary neo-Confucianism' – a twentieth-century movement that was, in a nutshell, a philosophical overhaul of Confucian philosophy for use in the modern era.

The emergent Confucian philosophy of the eighth century CE wasn't completely novel though with respect to earlier interpretations of the Way of Kongzi, nor was there only one form of it. As explained below, while one form was more in continuity with Xunzi's approach, another drew on an element of the earlier Confucian tradition that had been all but forgotten – namely, what was referred to in Chapter 4 as Mengzi's mysticism. Confucian thinkers linked Mengzi's claim about a common human endowment to ideas taken from both Daoism and Buddhism. These ideas didn't naturally fit together, which might explain why it took several centuries for neo-Confucianism to emerge as a comprehensive philosophical system. When it did, at its core was a theory about the evolution of the cosmos that would have been unrecognizable to Kongzi, Mengzi or Xunzi.

Inspired by the cosmological speculations of the *Yijing* (which at the time was believed to have been authored by Kongzi), neo-Confucian cosmology promoted the idea that all things exist in an original unity. The notion of original unity includes two distinct ideas. First the idea of chronological unity – this gives us a theory of cosmogenesis, according to which all things are derived from an original one thing. The second idea is logical rather than chronological – at the most fundamental level all things are One. Both of these ideas were important to neo-Confucians, although the second, logical, idea of original unity takes us closest to the heart of their concerns. Chinese Buddhists and Daoists had already popularized the notion of original unity in the context of their own philosophies. The challenge for Confucian thinkers was to integrate it into a genuinely Confucian world view; this was especially difficult because prior to this time Confucian scholars had displayed scant interest in such cosmological speculations.

This challenge was met in different ways by neo-Confucianism's two main schools. These schools were founded by two brothers who lived in the eleventh century CE. Cheng Yi (Ch'eng I, 1033–1107) started the school which became known as the School of Laws or Principles (*lixue*) and his slightly older sibling, Cheng Hao (Ch'eng Hao, 1032–85), started the other school: the School of Heart–Mind (*xinxue*). The philosophical controversy between these two schools shaped the development of all major forms of Chinese philosophy from the eleventh century to the modern period. The former school came to be referred to as the Cheng-Zhu school (after Cheng Yi and its principal later exponent Zhu Xi); the latter school is now sometimes referred to as the Lu-Wang school after its two most influential representatives – who we shall meet later in this chapter (see Ivanhoe 2009: 32). We explore the basic ideas of these two forms of neo-Confucianism in the following sections.

THE PROBLEM OF THE MANY AND THE ONE

Given their interest in theories of cosmogenesis and their exposure to Buddhist metaphysics, it is unsurprising that neo-Confucians (like some of the earlier philosophers in India, considered in Chapter 2) sought to explain the relationship between the plurality of objects in the world of our experience and the original unity which they held to be the more fundamental reality.

The School of Laws or Principles, which from now on we shall call the School of *Li*, sought to explain this relationship by taking up and elaborating ideas which had been advanced much earlier by the philosophers of the School of Names. The thinkers of the School of *Li* were interested in what was beyond shapes and features, which they identified with the *li* 理, 'principles' or 'laws' (despite having the same pronunciation, this is not the same word that was used by the earlier Confucians to refer to rites, ritual or propriety 禮). The *li* thus came to play the role in their theory that universals had occupied in Gongsun Long's view. The *li* of a thing was thought to be what determined that thing's nature. Everything that exists has a nature and so everything must have a *li*, or so the argument went. The *li* was thought to be inherent to the thing in the sense that a thing could not be what it was without its *li*. Moreover, the *li* was thought to enter the thing as soon as that thing began to exist. This understanding of the relationship between the particular thing and its universal, its *li*, was applied to artefacts as well as to natural objects.

A further idea taken from the School of Names is that *li* are absolute in the sense that they never cease to exist. In other words, *li* are eternal. One somewhat counter-intuitive implication of this is that the *li* of an artefact exists before the artefact has been invented. So, for example, before humans invented ships, the *li* of ships existed. When humans thought that they invented ships what they really did was discover the *li* of ships and bring about its instantiation (this example is from Fung 1976: 297).

The world of our experience is host to many kinds of objects, both natural objects and artefacts, and this suggests that there must be a very large number of *li*. If the theory of *li* is to be made consistent with the idea of original unity, then we need some account of how the many kinds of *li* are connected within the original unity. It was precisely to provide such an explanation that the philosophers associated with the School of *Li* introduced the notion of the Supreme Ultimate or *taiji* (*T'ai Chi*). Just as everything that exists within the cosmos has a *li* which constitutes its nature, so the universe itself must have a *li* which constitutes its nature. Zhu Xi (1130–1200), whom we met in Chapter 4, was responsible for introducing this idea. He claimed that the *Li* of the universe includes within itself the *li* of all things, and this is why he named it the Supreme Ultimate.

TRANSCENDENCE AND IMMANENCE

Zhu Xi characterized the Supreme Ultimate as the 'highest of all, beyond which nothing can be. It is the most high, most mystical, and most abstruse, surpassing everything' (Fung 1976: 297). Despite believing it to be transcendent to all individual objects, he held the Supreme Ultimate to be immanent within each individual existing thing. Explaining the idea of immanence, Zhu Xi wrote: 'With regard to heaven and earth in general, the Supreme Ultimate is in heaven and earth. And with regard to the myriad things in particular, the Supreme Ultimate is in every one of them too' (in ibid., p. 298). Indeed, the presence of the Supreme Ultimate in an individual thing was thought to be necessary for that thing's existence.

But this returns us to a now familiar problem. Given that the Supreme Ultimate is in every single existing thing, how can we explain its unity – the fact that it is one thing? Zhu Xi's proposed solution was that the Supreme Ultimate is immanent within each individual thing *in its entirety*. In other words, every individual thing contains within it the whole and undivided Supreme Ultimate! He illustrates this idea by comparing the Supreme Ultimate to 'the moon shining in the heavens, of which, though it is reflected in rivers and lakes and thus is everywhere visible, we would not therefore say that it is divided' (in ibid., p. 298). The key point made by the analogy is that just as the whole of the moon is reflected in many different pieces of water, so the whole of the Supreme Ultimate can be immanent within many different individuals. In this way Zhu Xi sought to explain the Supreme Ultimate as the original unity behind and within all phenomena.

Once that issue was settled the way was open to apply this theory about the Supreme Ultimate to the task of understanding human nature. One of the more startling but nonetheless obvious implications of Zhu Xi's theory is that the Supreme Ultimate is immanent in each human person. But Zhu Xi did not conclude from this that the way to knowledge of the Supreme Ultimate was through looking within. He believed that – unless one is a sage – what one finds within is a degraded form of the Supreme Ultimate that does not disclose its true nature, because the individual human mind is too impure to reflect it (just as a puddle with a roiled surface cannot give a clear and complete reflection of the moon). So rather than introspection, like his Confucian predecessor Xunzi, he recommended learning the classics and practising ritual as the means eventually leading to knowledge of the Supreme Ultimate. He also suggested that these could be supplemented by careful study of the individual *li* found within the natural world, although he did not provide an account of the method to be used (for a recent attempt at such a study, see Wade 2007).

Zhu Xi's contemporary and philosophical sparing partner, Lu Xiangshan (Lu Hsiang-shan, aka Lu Jiuyuan, 1139–93), while agreeing that the Supreme Ultimate was within, disagreed with Zhu Xi's views about how it might be known (see Ivanhoe 2009: 38–39; and S.-H. Liu 1998: chapter 9). He argued that each human being is capable of knowing the Supreme Ultimate through introspection, roughly understood as the activity of turning one's attention inward towards one's deepest self rather than outward towards the external world. Introspection was of great significance to the School of Heart–Mind (of which Lu Xiangshan is a principal representative). We now consider how this school attempted to explain the relationship between the one and the many.

INTROSPECTION

The idea of the oneness of all things was of vital importance to philosophers associated with the School of Heart–Mind. Cheng Hao, the School's founder, argued that the idea of original unity (in the logical, not the chronological, sense) was not alien to Confucianism, as many had assumed, but had instead been in the tradition from the earliest days. He claimed that this could be seen by re-examining the central Confucian concept '*ren*' (see Chapter 4). Cheng Hao explains:

> The student must first of all understand the nature of *ren*. The man of *ren* forms one body with all things without any differentiation. Righteousness, propriety, wisdom, and faithfulness are all [expressions of] *ren*. [One's duty] is to understand this principle (*li*) and preserve *ren* with sincerity and seriousness (*ching*), that is all. ... Nothing can be equal to this Way. ... It is so vast that nothing can adequately explain it. All operations of the universe are our operations. Mencius said that 'all things are already complete in oneself' and that one must 'examine oneself and be sincere (or absolutely real)' and only then will there be great joy. ... If one preserves it (*ren*) with this idea, what more is to be done? ... Not the slightest effort is exerted! This is the way to

> preserve *ren*. As *ren* is preserved, the self and the other are then identified.
>
> (In Chan 1973: 523f.; Chan uses *jen* not *ren*.)

The idea that all things are within each person is prominent in this passage, and the implication is drawn that it must be possible to arrive at knowledge of all things through looking within oneself. In other words, introspection (what in the *Mengzi* is described as 'pure knowing' *liangzhi*) is the key to knowledge of all things, not just of one's own mind (see Ivanhoe 2009: 105). However, a person who introspects does not only have access to knowledge of every individual thing; that person can also apprehend the original unity of all things. Such an apprehension is described by philosophers from the School of Heart–Mind as 'enlightenment'. Where these thinkers differ from those associated with the School of *Li* is in the crucial claim that the mind is *Li*. As Philip Ivanhoe explains, for Zhu Xi the heart–mind *contains* principles (i.e. *li*), while according to Lu Xiangshan in the School of Heart–Mind, the heart–mind *is* principle (i.e. *Li*) (see Ivanhoe 2009: 109). As Ivanhoe also points out, this explains the different approaches to the acquisition of knowledge recommended by the two schools.

Taking the idea that the heart–mind is *Li* one step further Lu Xiangshan argued that as *Li* was the universe, then the heart–mind is the universe. Thus he declared: 'The universe [i.e. space and time] is my heart–mind; my heart–mind is the universe' (in Ivanhoe 2009: 89).

The School of *Li* had proposed that the cosmos contains two kinds of existing things: *li* (in the sense of Gongsun Long's universals) and concrete individual things in which the *li* are immanent. In other words, they were dualists about the fundamental nature of reality. As we have seen, the School of Heart–Mind disagreed with this dualist conception of reality, holding instead that only one thing exists and that one thing is a universe in which there is a perfect correspondence between the *li* in the heart–mind and the *li* in the world. Lu Xiangshan taught that at the most fundamental level there was an identity between our thoughts and what there is in the world. His position does not involve a reduction of the world to the mind, although he has often been interpreted this way. Rather he is poised delicately between the two extremes of **idealism** and **materialism**. The next thinker we consider strove to maintain this balance, while taking the theory to an even higher level of refinement.

UNIVERSAL MIND

The most sophisticated exponent of the School of Heart–Mind was Wang Yangming (Wang Shou-jen, 1472–1529). The following passage is from his recorded sayings:

> The master was strolling in the mountains of Nan Zhen when a friend pointed to the flowering trees on a nearby cliff and said, 'If in all the world, there are no principles outside the heart–mind, what do you say about these flowering trees, which blossom and drop their flowers on their own, deep in the mountains? What have they to do with my heart–mind?'.
>
> The master said, 'Before you looked at these flowers, they along with your heart–mind had reverted to a state of stillness. When you came and looked upon these flowers, their colors became clear. This shows these flowers are not outside your heart–mind.'
>
> (Ivanhoe's translation 2009: 109; compare the translation in Fung 1976: 309.)

On the basis of passages like this one, Wang Yangming has often been interpreted as denying that the things which make up the universe exist independently of human minds (Fung interprets him this way). In other words, he is interpreted as an idealist who holds that the flowers only exist when a mind brings 'them' to attention. When the mind withdraws its awareness, the flowers no longer appear. Thus, on this interpretation, the mind determines which *li* are instantiated at any given moment thereby determining which individual things exist at that moment. To borrow a bureaucratic expression from Fung Yu-Lan, the mind legislates the *li*.

However, to interpret Wang Yangming as denying the mind-independent existence of the external world (as the Chinese counterpart of the British idealist philosopher Bishop Berkeley) does not do justice to the originality of his thought. Ivanhoe has convincingly argued for a more subtle interpretation of Wang Yangming's position according to which the heart–mind does not create the *li* but the *li* are nonetheless in the mind because of the original unity in which mind and *li* abide. (It may be that his position would be more akin to the western philosopher Spinoza's dual-aspect theory than to idealism.) Heart–mind and world are not external to each other but correspond in a unity in which neither can be reduced or eliminated (see Ivanhoe 2009: 101–15; and 2002).

Wang Yangming's claim that before his friend looked at the flowers both his mind and the flowers were in a 'state of stillness' might then be understood by deploying the notion of **secondary qualities**. Secondary qualities are things like colour and taste; they are qualities that seem to depend for their existence on our ability to perceive them. Wang Yangming can be interpreted as saying that the objects do not possess secondary qualities unless they are brought into relation with a perceiving mind. The flowers are not colourful in themselves, but only to a being with the right kind of perceptual apparatus. We might say that flowers in a 'state of stillness' have the potential to appear as colourful, but that potential is only actualized when a mind attends to them. The attention our minds give to the world, in interactions with the things constitutive of that world, produces the world of our experience. This is possible because of the correspondence between the *li* in our minds and the potential inherent within things.

Just as the School of *Li* philosophers were led to posit the Supreme Ultimate to explain the connection between the multitudinous *li*, the philosophers of the School of Heart–Mind were led to posit the Universal or Original Heart–Mind (*benxin*) to explain the connection between the multitude of individual heart–minds. Like the Buddha-nature championed by earlier Chinese Buddhists, the Original Heart–Mind was thought to be a universal human endowment. The sage was then understood to be someone whose access to the Original Heart–Mind was not hampered by impurities located in the individual heart–mind. One with such clearness of vision could act spontaneously according to the directions of the Original Heart–Mind.

The debt to earlier Buddhists' interpretations of the Buddha-nature, and especially to the Chan understanding of this, is nowhere more evident than here. In fact, these neo-Confucian ideas were such a departure from anything found in the earlier Confucian tradition that those promoting them had to work hard to establish continuity between their views and those of their predecessors. They were targeted by critics who accused them of propounding what was essentially a Buddhist philosophy under a thin veneer of Confucian terminology. The neo-Confucian School of Heart–Mind responded to this criticism by explaining that their ideas could be traced back to Mengzi's belief that human nature is innately good. Mengzi's example of the child about to fall into the well was reused in this new context to support the claim that we all have it in us to act in accordance with the Original Heart–Mind. Echoes of Mengzi's view can be seen in the following quote from Wang Yangming:

> The mind of man is Heaven. There is nothing that is not included in the mind of man. All of us are this single Heaven, but because of the obscurings caused by selfishness, the original state of heaven is not made manifest. Every time we extend our intuitive knowledge, we clear away the obscurings, and when all of them are cleared away, our original nature is restored, and we again become part of this Heaven. The intuitive knowledge of the part is the intuitive knowledge of the whole. The intuitive knowledge of the whole is the intuitive knowledge of the part. Everything is the single whole.
>
> (In Fung 1976: 315)

SAGELINESS

In this chapter we have traced a remarkable convergence of views drawn from a number of different traditions. Perhaps the most striking point of convergence concerns the understanding of sageliness found in the neo-Confucianism of the School of Heart–Mind and the conception of enlightenment developed by Huineng's Southern School of Chan Buddhism. Both schools argue that our minds are intrinsically pure and that the perfected person and the unperfected one share exactly the same universal endowment: the Buddha-nature or the Original Heart–Mind. The only difference between the perfected and the unperfected is that the former have unimpeded access to their original nature and the latter do not. The former reflect the universal as a clear mirror, whereas the latter do so like a muddy pool. But for both schools there is nothing extrinsic to the person that causes this lack of clarity, because both teach that there is no duality between the mind and the world. So if a person is not perfected the problem lies in their (heart–)mind. Hence both traditions developed meditative techniques and recommended similar pedagogical practices to rectify this situation. Both also followed the earlier Daoists in advising against elaborate spiritual practice – enlightenment was to be arrived at after the manner of Cook Ding, through mindful pursuit of practical activities. The peculiarly Confucian twist to this last piece of advice was to add that following the Way of Kongzi and living a life of Confucian virtue was the means to bring the Original Heart–Mind to full expression. Thus we have arrived at a form of Confucianism that has been reframed by its encounter with Buddhism and its assimilation of quintessentially Daoist themes.

SUMMARY OF CHAPTER 6

This chapter began with a discussion of the School of Names. Philosophers associated with this 'school' were particularly interested in the relations between, on the one hand, words and things, and on the other hand, individuals and universals. The discussion of universals led to an examination of the development of Chan Buddhist philosophy which held that at the core of all things lies a pure and undefiled Buddha-nature. This conviction led them to hold distinctive views about enlightenment, spiritual practice and pedagogy – views which revealed a debt to earlier Daoist philosophy, especially that of Zhuangzi.

We then saw how these ideas reappeared and were reworked into new systems of thought in the two main forms of neo-Confucian philosophy. The focus of the second part of the chapter was on how neo-Confucians such as Zhu Xi and Wang Yangming sought to explain the relationship between the plurality of objects in the world of our experience and the unity which was believed to be the more fundamental reality. Examining the way they handled this issue led to a discussion of their views on transcendence and immanence. Two branches of neo-Confucian philosophy were considered: the School of Laws or Principles and the School of Heart–Mind. Noting the importance given to introspection by thinkers belonging to the School of Heart–Mind brought us to the point where their thinking about the Original Heart–Mind converged with the Chan interpretation of the Buddha-nature.

REFERENCES AND FURTHER READING

PRIMARY TEXTS

Wing-tsit Chan (ed.), *A Sourcebook in Chinese Philosophy*, 4th edition (Princeton: Princeton University Press, 1973), chapter 23: *The Platform Sutra*.

Thomas Cleary (trans.), *The Sutra of Hui-neng: Grand Master of Zen* (Boston and London: Shambhala, 1998). Contains Hui-neng's commentary on the *Diamond Sūtra*.

Alexander Holstein (trans.), *Pointing at the Moon: 100 Zen Koans from Chinese Masters* (Rutland, Vermont and Tokyo, Japan: Charles E. Turtle Company, 1993).

Philip J. Ivanhoe (trans.), *Readings from the Lu-Wang School of Neo-Confucianism* (Indianapolis: Hackett, 2009). Indispensable for understanding neo-Confucianism, this book contains introductions and translations of *The Platform Sūtra* and selected material from Lu Xiangshan and Wang Yangming.

Philip J. Ivanhoe and Bryan W. Van Norden (eds), *Readings in Classical Chinese Philosophy*, 2nd edition (Indianapolis: Hackett, 2005). Contains Gongsun Long's essay 'On the White Horse' (pp. 363–68).

D. T. Suzuki (ed.), *Manual of Zen Buddhism* (New York: Grove Press, 1960). 'Bringing the Ox Home' is of particular interest.

SECONDARY LITERATURE

Cathy Cantwell, *Buddhism: The Basics* (London and New York: Routledge, 2010).

Yu-Lan Fung, *A Short History of Chinese Philosophy: A Systematic Account of Chinese Thought from Its Origin to the Present Day* (New York: The Free Press, 1976). See chapter 8 on the School of Names and chapter 15 on neo-Confucianism. The book is also available in a two-volume edition (Princeton: Princeton University Press, 1983).

Philip J. Ivanhoe, *Ethics in the Confucian Tradition: The Thought of Mengzi and Wang Yangming* (Indianapolis: Hackett, 2002).

JeeLoo Liu, *An Introduction to Chinese Philosophy: From Ancient Philosophy to Chinese Buddhism* (Oxford: Blackwell, 2006), especially chapter 12.

Shu-Hsien Liu, *Understanding Confucian Philosophy: Classical and Sung-Ming* (Westport, Connecticut and London: Praeger, 1998).

Bryan W. Van Norden and *Introduction to Classical Chinese Philosophy* (Indianapolis: Hackett, 2011).

David Wade, *Li: Dynamic Form in Nature* (Glastonbury: Wooden Books, 2007).

Jan Westerhoff, *Nāgārjuna's Madhyamaka: A Philosophical Introduction* (Oxford: OUP, 2009).

Paul Williams, *Mahāyāna Buddhism: The Doctrinal Foundations* (London and New York: Routledge, 1989).

Arthur F. Wright, *Buddhism in Chinese History* (Stanford, CA: Stanford University Press, 1959).

CONCLUSION

This book has introduced a wide range of philosophies from both India and China. Despite the diversity on exhibit here, I contend that it still makes sense to regard Indian philosophies and Chinese philosophies as belonging to two separate philosophical 'families'. Earlier I explained why this is so by referring to the Vedic root and the Sinitic root out of which Indian and Chinese philosophies, respectively, emerged. I will now briefly suggest another, complimentary, way of thinking about what distinguishes these two Asian philosophical families while simultaneously uniting the diverse traditions within each one.

The Indian and Chinese philosophical families developed and matured around different conceptual metaphors, each leading to a particular understanding of both the practice and the goal of philosophy. George Lakoff and Mark Johnson introduced the notion of a conceptual metaphor to refer to those metaphors that organize whole networks of thought, experience and activity. They illustrate how these metaphors work with the example of one that has played a key role in western thought, that of 'argument as war'. Commenting on the way this metaphor is used, they write:

> It is important to see that we don't just *talk* about arguments in terms of war. We can actually win or lose arguments. We see the person we are arguing with as an opponent. We attack his positions and we defend

> our own. We gain and lose ground. We plan and use strategies. If we find a position indefensible, we can abandon it and take a new line of attack. Many of the things we *do* in arguing are partially structured by the concept of war. Though there is no physical battle, there is a verbal battle, and the structure of an argument – attack, defense, counterattack, etc. – reflects this. It is in this sense that the ARGUMENT IS WAR metaphor is one that we live by in this [i.e. western] culture; it structures the actions we perform in arguing.
>
> (Lakoff and Johnson 1980: 75)

The 'argument is war' metaphor generates an understanding of the practice of philosophy as engagement in a battle. This in turn engenders a portrayal of the goal of philosophy as being to win the battle, or – in other words – the argument. Now, this particular conceptual metaphor did not have a structuring role for the philosophies of India or those of China. We can, however, identify other metaphors which do seem to have enjoyed a similarly far-reaching impact on the structure of these Asian philosophies as that exercised by the 'argument is war' metaphor upon western thought.

Philosophy in ancient and classical India was structured according to the dominant conceptual metaphor of sight. As mentioned earlier, in Sanskrit the word '*darśana*' is derived from the verbal root 'to see'. The philosopher's model was the ancient seer, whose vision was reflected in the Vedic literature. Consequently, philosophy was practised in order to clear away the obstacles to a true vision of the genuine reality lying behind the way things appear to us. Given that the philosopher's goal was to arrive at the correct perspective (*darśana*) from which things could be seen as they really are, philosophical disagreement focused on the issue of which perspective was the most revealing. Testing these rival perspectives in the open context of public debate was thus central to the practice of philosophy in classical India. The logical culmination of this trend, as we saw in Chapter 1, was the Jaina's development of a method which was able to incorporate apparently rival perspectives within a larger vision.

Appealing to the distinction introduced in Chapter 5, we can say that insofar as philosophers in India sought knowledge about the nature of reality, they sought 'knowledge that' rather than 'knowledge how'. Matters were otherwise in classical China, and one of the explanations for this difference might be that in China the practice of philosophy was structured by a different metaphor. There the dominant conceptual metaphor was Dao – the Way. Philosophers sought a way of living within this world rather than knowledge of a supposed deeper reality behind the world of our experience. Their model was the Sage-King who combined personal virtue with wisdom and the ability to rule well. Despite the Confucian emphasis on scholarship, and with the exception of thinkers associated with the School of Names, the philosophies of classical China were united in their pursuit of the Way. They were overwhelmingly concerned with 'knowledge how' rather than 'knowledge that'. Neither merely winning an argument nor arriving at an objectively correct but abstract understanding of the world were the main goals of philosophical activity in China.

Obviously these are generalizations, and generalizations can be dangerous in this field of study if they cause exceptions to be overlooked. I have already mentioned the School of Names as an exception to the main trend followed by classical Chinese philosophers. In their relentless pursuit of the conclusion of an argument, no matter how counter-intuitive that conclusion might seem, Gongsun Long and Hui Shi followed a similar argumentative strategy to that employed by the Indian Cārvākas in a later era. Whereas within the Indian milieu the contribution of the Cārvākas was assimilated into the wider philosophical discussion and played a key role in spurring a number of philosophical developments within other *darśanas*, in China the contribution of the School of Names seems to have had the opposite effect. One possible explanation for this might be that these thinkers were simply unable to participate fully in the philosophical culture that was developing because their understanding of philosophy was not structured by the conceptual metaphor of Dao that informed that culture. In fact, as explained in Chapter 6, the work of the thinkers associated with the School of Names contributed to the disaffection with rigorous philosophical argumentation and the distrust of language which characterized China's post-classical philosophies.

In India the Yoga *darśana* might also seem to constitute an exception. As explained in Chapter 2, the interests of this school were primarily practical and the *Yoga Sūtra* is concerned to teach a technique. However, the practical advice provided by this *darśana* does not purport to tell the yoga practitioner how to flourish within this world, rather it teaches her to disengage from the world by refining the vehicle that gives us a clear vision of what lies beyond.

Despite the differences between the philosophies of India and those of China that, as we have seen, are partially the result of the particular conceptual metaphors which structure them, there remains some commonality that can be uncovered by attending to the kinds of questions and concerns that philosophical inquiry within each context revolved around. In both India and China philosophers were concerned to understand the world of our experience. In India this led to a metaphysical inquiry that purported to inform us about the deeper reality beyond the world of experience. In China, by contrast, philosophical speculation was harnessed to address the practical challenges of moral improvement and good governance. When classical Chinese thinkers did allow their speculations to become more abstract, they still never lost sight of the vital and persistent connection between the ultimately real Dao (the unhewn wood of the *Daodejing*) and the world of our experience.

Likewise, in both India and China, philosophers were keen to investigate human personhood. In India this investigation focused on attaining the correct viewpoint that would yield an accurate account of the nature of the true self underlying experience – with a view to the final liberation of that true self from the cycle of rebirth. In China, the concern was to understand human nature in order to learn how to deliver effective moral education and how best to govern the state – and, even more basically, how to live a good life.

In Chapter 6 we surveyed the encounter between Indian and Chinese philosophies that was set in train by the transmission of Buddhism from India to China. As explained in that chapter, Chan Buddhism and neo-Confucianism both evolved from that encounter. In each of them a fusion can be discerned of the two conceptual metaphors dominant within the philosophies of Asia (that is, philosophy as seeking vision and philosophy as seeking the Way). In Chan, what the enlightened one sees is nothing other than the world of our everyday experience; and Chan practice is designed to facilitate that unobstructed vision. The neo-Confucians, likewise, combined that view with the insight that the *li* – the ultimate nature of things – was available to us directly through our experience. The person living according to the Way has become perfected and has access to the deeper reality because his inner and outer experience is in complete harmony with it. It is no accident that the neo-Confucians adopted the term 'enlightenment', reflecting the impact of the vision metaphor that was dominant in India, but they understood it to refer to a 'vision of the Dao'. Combining these two metaphors thus gave rise to a new one which to some degree blended the theoretical and practical aspects of philosophy. The new metaphor was: seeing the Way.

UNEXPLORED TERRAIN

This book has sought to provide the reader with a guide to the contours of the main philosophical traditions of India and China; as such it has inevitably left much ground unexplored. In particular, space has not permitted discussion of recent developments within those Chinese and Indian philosophies which have continued to evolve into the twenty-first century (although reading suggestions are provided at the end of this chapter) or of the various fruitful encounters that have taken place between Asian philosophies and western thought. The Japanese **Kyoto School**, for example, made a distinctive contribution to western philosophy in the twentieth century by bringing Buddhism into dialogue with both Neoplatonism and modern German philosophy. Indian and Chinese philosophies are currently contributing to areas of global philosophical and cultural concern (for instance, Confucian philosophy is impacting western moral philosophy, especially virtue ethics; Daoism is informing environmental philosophy; and Buddhism is expanding our understanding of the relation between philosophy and science).

Another story hinted at but left untold by this short book is that of the deep and lasting impact of some of the philosophies considered here within other parts of Asia. In particular, exploring the history of Buddhism and Confucianism within Japan and Korea would be a natural follow-up to the material introduced here (again, reading suggestions are included below), as would be an investigation of Tibetan Buddhist philosophy.

GLOBAL PHILOSOPHY

Earlier I mentioned that the notion of global philosophy remains something of a Holy Grail among practitioners of the modern discipline of comparative philosophy. It seems appropriate to end this book by briefly returning to this notion.

A so-called 'global philosophy' that attempted to merge the various philosophies of the world into a common tradition seems unlikely to succeed. Moreover, given what was said above about the way that the philosophical traditions of China, India and those of the West are structured by different conceptual metaphors, it is improbable that these traditions could be coherently merged. Instead of pursuing the chimera of this reductive form of a global philosophy, then, it seems more promising to focus on the idea of a global philosopher – one who is conversant with a number of the world's philosophical traditions and is equipped to participate in philosophical discussion within and between them.

Insofar as they were pioneers of a non-reductive form of philosophical pluralism, the philosophers of classical India provide us with a model here. The *darśanas* were distinct yet dependent upon each other for the stimulus that led to growth. In some cases one *darśana* would simply adopt the view of another on some particular issue, as, for example, the Yoga *darśana* adopted the Sāṁkhya ontology. But the philosophers belonging to these *darśanas* were each engaged in a common search for truth. Although the *āstika darśanas* and the *nāstika darśanas* had some fundamental disagreements, members of each were able to participate fully in the intellectual culture of their day.

The Jainas grasped the idea that irreducibly different philosophical perspectives could all contribute to our understanding, as, in another cultural context, did the Daoist thinker Zhuangzi. The same can be said about philosophical traditions that are shaped by different conceptual metaphors. As suggested above, it is because of the role such metaphors have played that we are able so easily to identify otherwise diverse philosophies as belonging to the same family, or not. Such traditions are not saying the same thing in different ways, and they might practice philosophy in diverse ways and with different goals. Nonetheless each can make a valuable contribution to our understanding of the questions which arise from reflection upon our shared world and the experiences which are common to us.

REFERENCES AND FURTHER READING

Choi Min-Hong, *A Modern History of Korean Philosophy* (Seoul: Seong Moon SA, 1980).

Chung-Ying Cheng and Nicholas Bunnin (eds), *Contemporary Chinese Philosophy* (Oxford: Blackwell, 2002).

J. J. Clarke, *Oriental Enlightenment: The Encounter between Asian and Western Thought* (London and New York: Routledge, 1997). A fascinating exploration of the impact of Asian ideas on the philosophy, religion, psychology and science of the West.

——, *The Tao of the West: Western Transformations of Taoist Thought* (London and New York: Routledge, 2000). This prize-winning book not only serves as an introduction to Daoism but is essential reading for understanding its impact on western thought.

David A. Dilworth and Valdo H. Vigielmo, with A. J. Zavala (edited and translated), *Sourcebook for Modern Japanese Philosophy: Selected Documents* (Westport, Connecticut and London: Greenwood Press, 1998).

Peter H. Lee and Wm. Theodore de Bary (eds), *Sources of Korean Tradition*. Volume 1: *From Early Times to the Sixteenth Century* (New York: Columbia University Press, 1997).

George Lakoff and Mark Johnson, *Metaphors We Live By* (Chicago: University of Chicago Press, 1980).

Bimal Krishna Matilal, *Logic, Language and Reality: Indian Philosophy and Contemporary Issues* (Delhi: Motilal Banarsidass, 1990).

Wm. Theodore de Bary, et al. (eds), *Sources of Japanese Tradition*. Volume 1: *From Early Times to the Sixteenth Century* (New York: Columbia University Press, 2001).

Richard E. Nisbett, *The Geography of Thought: How Asians and Westerners Think Differently … and Why* (New York, London, Toronto, Sydney: Free Press, 2003). Nisbett employs cognitive psychology to shed light on the cultural differences underlying the different approaches to abstract thinking found in China and the West.

APPENDIX 1
TIMELINES

INDIA

*c.*2500–1800 BCE	Indus Valley Civilization.
*c.*1500–300 BCE	Brahmanical or Vedic Period.
	Ṛg Veda, *c.*1500 BCE
	Sāma Veda
	Yajur Veda
	Atharva Veda
	Brāhmaṇas, *c.*1000 BCE
	Āraṇyakas, *c.*900 BCE
	Upaniṣad, *c.*800–300 BCE
599–527 BCE	Māhavīra, the 'founder' of Jainism.
*c.*485–405 BCE	Siddhartha Gotama, the Buddha (traditional dates: 563–483 BCE)
350–150 BCE	Buddhist Period.
Third–second century BCE	Collaboration between Vaiśeṣika and Nyāya.
	Evolution of the Buddhist Abhidharma tradition.
	Kaṇāda's *Vaiśeṣika Sūtra.*
First century BCE	*Vedānta* or *Brahma Sūtra* (traditionally attributed to Bādarāyaṇa).
First century BCE–First century CE	Mahāyāna Buddhism emerges.
Circa second century CE	Nāgārjuna's *Madhyamaka Kārikā.*

Third century CE	Gotama's *Nyāya Sūtra*.
	Pūrva Mīmāṁsā Sūtra.
	Yoga Sūtra (traditionally attributed to Patañjali).
350–500 CE	Classical 'Hindu' Period.
	Final redaction of epics: *Mahābhārata* and *Rāmāyana*. (The *Bhagavad-gītā*, *c.*200 BCE, is included in the *Mahābhārata*.)
Fourth century	Ascendancy of the Yogācāra (Mind Only) school of Buddhism.
Fourth or fifth century CE	Yogācārin philosopher Vasubandhu.
Fourth–fifth century CE	Īśvarakṛṣṇa's *Sāṃkhya Kārikā*.
Fifth century CE	The grammarian Bhartṛhari (influenced the Mīmāṁsā school).
Seventh century CE	Peak of the Mīmāṁsā.
	The *Tattvopaplavasiṃha* (*The Lion of Destruction of Philosophical Theories*) authored by the Cārvāka Jayarāśi.
Eighth century CE	Śaṇkara's school of Advaita Vedānta.
Eleventh century CE	Rāmānuja's Viśiṣṭādvaita Vedānta (qualified non-dualism).
500–1000 CE	Tantric era (Hindu and Buddhist).
Fourteenth century CE	Mādhava's *Sarvadarśanasaṃgraha*.

CHINA

See also the text box, 'Periods and dynasties up to the Qin', in the Introduction, p. 15.

*c.*600–200 BCE	*The classical era. Key figures:*
	Kongzi 551–479 BCE.
	Laozi (Lao Tzu) traditionally regarded as contemporary with Kongzi.
	Yang Zhu (Yang Chu) *c.*440–360 BCE. A proto-Daoist.
	Mozi (Mo-tzu) *c.*480–390 BCE. Founder of Mohism.
	Zhuangzi (Chuang Tzu) *c.*369–286 BCE. Daoist.
	Mengzi (Mencius) *c.*371–289 BCE. Confucian.
	Hui Shi (Hui Shih) *c.*380–305 BCE. School of Names.
	Gongsun Long (Kung-sun Lung) born *c.*380 BCE. School of Names.
	Xunzi (Hsün-tzu) *c.*340–245 BCE. Confucian.
	Han Feizi *c.*280–233 BCE. Legalist.

Qin dynasty 221–207 BCE	
Han dynasty 206 BCE to 220 CE	
470–534 CE	Bodhidharma (traditional dates). First Patriarch of Chan Buddhism.
601–74 CE	Hongren (Hung-jen). Fifth Patriarch of Chan Buddhism.
*c.*606–706 CE	Shenxiu (Shen-hsiu). Head of the Northern School of Chan.
Tang dynasty 618–906 CE	
638–713 CE	Huineng. Head of the Southern School of Chan and later the Sixth Patriarch.
670–762 CE	Shenhui. Huineng's disciple.
Eighth century CE	Emergence of neo-Confucianism.
*c.*810–66 CE	Lin Ji (Yi-hsüan). A Chan Master.
Song dynasty 960–1279 CE	
Eleventh century CE	Maturity of neo-Confucianism.
1032–85 CE	Cheng Hao (Ch'eng Hao). Founder of the neo-Confucian School of Heart–Mind.
1033–1107 CE	Cheng Yi (Ch'eng I). Founder of the neo-Confucian School of Laws or Principles.
1130–1200 CE	Zhu Xi (Chu Hsi). Key figure in the School of Laws or Principles.
1139–93 CE	Lu Xiangshan (Lu Hsiang-shan, aka Lu Jiuyuan). Key figure in the School of Heart–Mind (Lu-Wang neo-Confucianism).
Yuan dynasty 1280–1367 CE	
Ming dynasty 1368–1643 CE	
1472–1529 CE	Wang Yangming (Wang Shou-jen). Leading neo-Confucian in the School of Heart–Mind (Lu-Wang neo-Confucianism).

APPENDIX 2
WEBSITES

Stanford Encyclopedia of Philosophy:
http://plato.stanford.edu/

This provides high-quality scholarly articles on the main topics and figures in western and Asian philosophy. Search the index for the philosophers covered in this book. Where a word appears in boldface in the main text of this book, that signifies that it can be looked up in this encyclopedia.

Karl Potter's *Encyclopaedia of Indian Philosophies*, volume 1, bibliography:
http://faculty.washington.edu/kpotter/

ACPA (Association of Chinese Philosophers in America):
www.acpa-net.org/index.html

A website devoted to the Indus Valley Civilization featuring a plethora of images and a range of recent scholarship:
www.harappa.com/har/har0.html

Thomas McEvilley talks about his book *The Shape of Ancient Thought*, in which he traces the sphere of influence that shaped both ancient Greece and ancient India:
http://video.google.com/videoplay?docid=4553155406381622401#

In this video he also explains the cultural significance of the serpents entwined in caduceus form (see Figure 5.2, on p. 151).

Chad Hansen's Chinese Philosophy Page:
www.philosophy.hku.hk/ch/

This site contains a wealth of interpretive material and resources on classical Chinese philosophy.

Buddhist, Confucian and Daoist e-texts, Indexes and Bibliographies (also containing links to Indian material):
www.acmuller.net/digitexts.html

Essential Readings on Chinese Philosophy:
http://faculty.vassar.edu/brvannor/bibliography.html

Compiled by Bryan W. Van Norden, this site lists essential readings under key thinkers or topics in classical and post-classical Chinese philosophy. It also contains links to other resources.

Timeline for China to 1700 noting key events in politics, society and culture, and including many individuals and movements:
www.indiana.edu/~e232/Time1.html

On Sanskrit: *www.omniglot.com/writing/sanskrit.htm*

On Pāli: *www.omniglot.com/writing/pali.htm*

On the Chinese script and language: *www.omniglot.com/writing/chinese.htm*

APPENDIX 3
PRONUNCIATION

The following highlights the main sounds that English speakers might have trouble with.

CHINESE *(PINYIN)*

Q is pronounced 'ch' (as in church). *Qin* is pronounced as 'chin'.

X is pronounced as an aspirated 's' (as in sheet). *Xun* (as in Xunzi) is pronounced as 'shun'.

Zh is pronounced as 'j' before a vowel (as in jade). *Zhou* is pronounced as 'joe'.

SANSKRIT

A bar over a letter indicates that it has a long sound. E.g., 'ā' is long (as in nirvāṇa), while 'a' is short (as in h*u*t).

i	as in h*i*t	ī	as in f*ee*t
u	as in p*u*t	ū	as in b*oo*t
e	like the *a* in may		
o	like the *o* in rope		
ṛ	like the *r* in pretty		
s	like the *s* in sit	ś, ṣ	both pronounced as 'sh'

ñ	as *ny* in canyon
t	as in *t*ea
ṭ	similar to *t* but with the tongue at the back of the palate
ṃ	sounded as *ng*, as in ha*ng*
ṅ, ṇ	as in *n*ot

GENERAL BIBLIOGRAPHY

CHINA

Wing-tsit Chan (ed.), *A Sourcebook in Chinese Philosophy*, 4th edition (Princeton: Princeton University Press, 1973). The most comprehensive available anthology.

Philip J. Ivanhoe and Bryan W. Van Norden (eds), *Readings in Classical Chinese Philosophy*, 2nd edition (Indianapolis: Hackett, 2005). Contains lucid translations of texts from major philosophers of the classical period.

Yu-lan Fung, *A History of Chinese Philosophy* (Princeton: Princeton University Press, 1983), 2 volumes, translated by Derk Bodde. A comprehensive introduction to the subject.

Wm. Theodore de Bary and Irene Bloom (eds), *Sources of Chinese Traditions: From Earliest Times to 1600* (New York: Columbia University Press, 1999).

INDIA

Sarandranath N. Dasgupta, *A History of Indian Philosophy*, 5 volumes (Cambridge: CUP, 1922–55).

Karl Potter (ed.), *Encyclopedia of Indian Philosophies*, 8 volumes (Delhi: Motilal Banarsidass, 1983–). An ongoing project with more volumes under preparation. Volume 1 comprises a comprehensive bibliography of the field. The volumes are also available online (see Appendix 2).

Sarvepalli Radhakrishnan and Charles A. Moore (eds), *A Sourcebook in Indian Philosophy* (Princeton: Princeton University Press, 1989).

WORLD PHILOSOPHY

Brian Carr and Indira Mahalingam (eds), *Companion Encyclopedia of Asian Philosophy* (London and New York: Routledge, 2001).
Eliot Deutsch and Ron Bontekoe (eds), *A Companion to World Philosophies* (Oxford: Blackwell, 1999).

SCHOLARLY JOURNALS

Asian Philosophy
Comparative and Continental Philosophy
Dao: A Journal of Comparative Philosophy
Journal of Chinese Philosophy
Journal of Indian and Buddhist Studies
Journal of Indian Philosophy
Philosophy East and West

INDEX

Note: **bold** numbers denote words found in text boxes and tables.